# The
# RESILIENT
# WARRIOR

*Tackling PTSD from a 30 Year*
*Police Officer Veteran*

## BY MICHAEL MORGAN

Edited by Lil Barcaski

Published by: GWN Publishing
www.GWNPublishing.com

Cover Design: Kristina Conatser

ISBN: 978-1-965971-33-8

# DEDICATION

*This book is dedicated to the men and women who ran toward the chaos, held the line when it mattered most, and are still fighting battles no one else can see.*

*You're not broken. You're human.*

*I see you – because I've been you*

# TABLE OF CONTENTS

Endorsements . . . . . . . . . . . . . . . . . . . . . . . . . . . . . . . . . . . . . . . . . . . . . . . 7

Foreword . . . . . . . . . . . . . . . . . . . . . . . . . . . . . . . . . . . . . . . . . . . . . . . . 13

Introduction . . . . . . . . . . . . . . . . . . . . . . . . . . . . . . . . . . . . . . . . . . . . 15

Chapter 1 . . . . . . . . . . . . . . . . . . . . . . . . . . . . . . . . . . . . . . . . . . . . . . . 19

Chapter 2 . . . . . . . . . . . . . . . . . . . . . . . . . . . . . . . . . . . . . . . . . . . . . . . 23

Chapter 3 . . . . . . . . . . . . . . . . . . . . . . . . . . . . . . . . . . . . . . . . . . . . . . . 29

Chapter 4 . . . . . . . . . . . . . . . . . . . . . . . . . . . . . . . . . . . . . . . . . . . . . . . 35

Chapter 5 . . . . . . . . . . . . . . . . . . . . . . . . . . . . . . . . . . . . . . . . . . . . . . . 39

Chapter 6 . . . . . . . . . . . . . . . . . . . . . . . . . . . . . . . . . . . . . . . . . . . . . . . 43

Chapter 7 . . . . . . . . . . . . . . . . . . . . . . . . . . . . . . . . . . . . . . . . . . . . . . . 49

Chapter 8 . . . . . . . . . . . . . . . . . . . . . . . . . . . . . . . . . . . . . . . . . . . . . . . 51

Chapter 9 . . . . . . . . . . . . . . . . . . . . . . . . . . . . . . . . . . . . . . . . . . . . . . . 57

Chapter 10 . . . . . . . . . . . . . . . . . . . . . . . . . . . . . . . . . . . . . . . . . . . . . . 63

Chapter 11 . . . . . . . . . . . . . . . . . . . . . . . . . . . . . . . . . . . . . . . . . . . . . . 67

Chapter 12 . . . . . . . . . . . . . . . . . . . . . . . . . . . . . . . . . . . . . . . . . . . . . . 73

Chapter 13 . . . . . . . . . . . . . . . . . . . . . . . . . . . . . . . . . . . . . . . . . . . . . . 77

Chapter 14 . . . . . . . . . . . . . . . . . . . . . . . . . . . . . . . . . . . . . . . . . . . . . . 81

Chapter 15 . . . . . . . . . . . . . . . . . . . . . . . . . . . . . . . . . . . . . . . . . . . . . . 89

Chapter 16 . . . . . . . . . . . . . . . . . . . . . . . . . . . . . . . . . . . . . . . . . . . . *95*

Chapter 17 . . . . . . . . . . . . . . . . . . . . . . . . . . . . . . . . . . . . . . . . . *101*

Chapter 18 . . . . . . . . . . . . . . . . . . . . . . . . . . . . . . . . . . . . . . . . . *109*

Chapter 19 . . . . . . . . . . . . . . . . . . . . . . . . . . . . . . . . . . . . . . . . . *113*

Chapter 20 . . . . . . . . . . . . . . . . . . . . . . . . . . . . . . . . . . . . . . . . . *121*

Chapter 21 . . . . . . . . . . . . . . . . . . . . . . . . . . . . . . . . . . . . . . . . . *125*

Chapter 22 . . . . . . . . . . . . . . . . . . . . . . . . . . . . . . . . . . . . . . . . . *129*

Chapter 23 . . . . . . . . . . . . . . . . . . . . . . . . . . . . . . . . . . . . . . . . . *141*

Chapter 24 . . . . . . . . . . . . . . . . . . . . . . . . . . . . . . . . . . . . . . . . . *145*

Chapter 25 . . . . . . . . . . . . . . . . . . . . . . . . . . . . . . . . . . . . . . . . . *149*

Chapter 26 . . . . . . . . . . . . . . . . . . . . . . . . . . . . . . . . . . . . . . . . . *157*

Chapter 27 . . . . . . . . . . . . . . . . . . . . . . . . . . . . . . . . . . . . . . . . . *163*

Acknowledgments . . . . . . . . . . . . . . . . . . . . . . . . . . . . . . . . . . . *167*

About the Author . . . . . . . . . . . . . . . . . . . . . . . . . . . . . . . . . . . *169*

# ENDORSEMENTS

There are certain people who step into your life and immediately radiate a presence you can feel a power, an integrity, an alignment that hits you in the soul.

The kind of presence that doesn't need to be explained... only recognized. Mike is one of those men. A true kindred spirit.

He served his country and his communities with honor wearing the badge in both New York and Atlanta, standing on the front lines where most people will never stand. He carried the weight, the trauma, and the battles that come with being a protector... and he fought his way through it with the heart of a warrior.

And now, after walking through the fire, Mike has become something even greater a beacon of healing, rebirth, and unshakable strength.

His message hits you. His energy lifts you. His journey reminds us all what's possible when a man refuses to break.

I'm truly blessed to call Mike a friend, a brother, and a teammate.

Some people come into your life for a season, But the ones cut from this cloth? They're tethered to your spirit for a divine reason!

**Gareth Hoernel**, Founder/CEO
GTH Consulting Group

Mike Morgan's powerful book must be read by every veteran and first responder because it shatters the myth that strength lives in silence. Mike lives the life of a warrior. He is a heavily muscled, heavily tatted, shaved-head protector who served for thirty years, stepping up to the plate multiple times when paying the ultimate price was a distinct possibility. Yet, his now transparent journey reveals that his dedication to the suck it up ethos led him down a path of deep emotional suppression, culminating in an explosion of anger, rage, addiction, and the crisis of Post-Traumatic Stress.

Mike Morgan has earned the instant credibility necessary to speak into this world. Mike's healing journey, a model of radical vulnerability, is a courageous blueprint that proves the most dangerous words are I'm fine, and that vulnerability is the gateway to unbelievable strength. This book is a vital, uncompromising guide from a man who survived the monsters, his own shadow, and now boldly shows others how to find their new purpose.

**Doug White**, Author of *Hiding in Plain Sight*

I initially met Michael Morgan, (aka Morgs), over 20 years ago when we both played for the Police/Fire Ice Hockey team in metro Atlanta. To say this team was made up of a bunch of characters would be extremely insufficient. Morgs was one of our founders and the Captain of this band of brothers. We had players from both police and fire departments and most of us were players from up north, aka New York and Pennsylvania. I immediately took a liking to Morgs as he was loud, obnoxious, partied hard, so therefore very similar to myself. But Mike was both a warrior and leader back then, and that was what drew me towards him. Morgs brought it every game and did not take any shifts off. Like myself, he hated to lose, and our practices were as intense as our games.

Morgs eventually moved away for his dream job in New York and the team eventually fell apart as did our conversations. I was scrolling on social media a few years back and said, "Is that Morgs on a reel?" I showed my wife as well and we both confirmed, holy shit, it's Morgs! I reached out to him on a DM and he immediately called my cell phone. We hit it off like family members do, never missing a beat. We both shared our healing journeys, and I sent him a copy of my book. Here is where our friendship has reunited and become stronger than ever. We both dropped the ego and macho BS, as both had gotten very real with our lives with the darkness almost taking the two of us away. Morgs has helped me since then become a better man and better person then I could have imagined. Through his podcast and our personal talks, he has helped me look even deeper into my healing journey and find gratitude in the simplest moments of life. Our darkness and many fatalities are not sadness and burdens anymore, they were a gift. Morgs helped me transform my own trauma into actual victories and I am beyond proud to call him a brother. Keep it up Morgs, the world is waiting to see what you accomplish next.

**Dennis Pishock**, Milton, Ga. Police
Officer, Author of *Angels and Demons*

There are very few people in life who truly understand what resilience means. Not the kind that gets posted on social media or spoken about in highlight reels, but the kind that is built in silence, in loss, in suffering, in long nights, where no one is watching and quitting would be easier than continuing.

Michael Morgan is one of those people.

I've known Michael not just as a friend, but as a brother. I've watched him endure moments that would have broken and crumbled most people, and instead of becoming bitter or hardened in the wrong ways, he chose to become stronger, more disciplined, and more grounded. That choice, made repeatedly over time, is what defines a resilient warrior, and it's the foundation of everything written in his book.

The Resilient Warrior is not a collection of motivational quotes or surface-level advice. It's a reflection of a life lived under pressure and a mindset forged through adversity.

Every chapter carries the weight of experience, lessons learned the hard way, truths discovered through struggle, and principles that only reveal themselves when comfort is stripped away.

What I respect most about Michael is his humility. He doesn't position himself as someone who has it all figured out. Instead, he writes as a man who has been tested, who has fallen, who has had to rebuild himself more than once, and who understands that resilience isn't about never breaking, but about learning how to put yourself back together with more intention and strength than before. Leaning on your small support circle around you to carry your weight.

This book speaks to anyone who has faced failure, loss, self-doubt, or the feeling of being overwhelmed by life's weight. It speaks to men and women who know that something inside them needs to change, but don't want empty motivation or false confidence.

Michael offers something far more valuable: clarity, accountability, and the courage to confront yourself honestly.

There is a quiet strength in these pages. A reminder that resilience is not loud. It doesn't need validation. It's built through discipline, consistency, and the willingness to keep moving forward even when the path is unclear. That message reflects the man I know; steady, principled, and relentless in his commitment to becoming better.

Michael Morgan lives the values he writes about. He shows up. He takes responsibility. He doesn't look for excuses, and he doesn't shy away from hard conversations. Especially the ones we must have with ourselves. That authenticity is what makes The Resilient Warrior resonate so deeply.

I am proud to stand behind his book, not because of its title or its message alone, but because I know the man who wrote it.

Michael is a warrior in the truest sense. Someone who speaks his words backed from heartache and lessons learned, someone who speaks from his soul, someone who has an open heart & mind.

If you are searching for a book that challenges you to rise, to endure, and to rebuild with purpose, there is no need to look any further. The Resilient Warrior will meet you where you are and demand more of who you choose to become.

With respect and brotherhood

**Zack Ferguson**, Former Navy SEAL,
Co-Owner: Defense Strategies Group,
Co-Founder: DSG Training Center

The Resilient Warrior is the powerful true story of Michael Morgan, a 30-year police officer who spent decades absorbing the trauma most people never see. Like so many first responders, he carried the weight quietly, believing duty meant endurance. But when the darkness grew too heavy, Michael chose a different path. Through the healing power of entheogenic sacraments, he confronted his pain, rediscovered his soul, and emerged transformed.

This book isn't just about survival. It's about awakening.

Michael now lives as a man who leads with his heart, grounded in truth, compassion, and service. And instead of climbing out alone, he is putting the ladder down for others - showing fellow warriors that they are not broken, that healing is possible, and that they, too, can return home.

A courageous journey. A needed voice. A guide for every hero carrying invisible wounds.

**Matthew "Whiz" Buckley**, Former Navy FA-18
Top Gun Fighter Pilot, Founder: No Fallen Heroes
Foundation, Founder: Sacred Warrior Fellowship

As a retired Fire Lieutenant with 20 plus years on the job and the founder of Operation Yellow Tape, I've met countless first responders. Few have impacted me the way Michael Morgan has. His 30 years in law enforcement have given him a raw, honest perspective on the mental health battles we all face behind the badge. His new book is more than stories. It's a lifeline, a reminder that strength is found in vulnerability, and that healing is possible when we stop suffering in silence. It's a powerful reminder of what we bring to this profession from our childhood before the trauma inside the yellow tape hammers our minds.

Since the day I met him, he has pushed me to grow, to speak openly, and to keep fighting for our brothers and sisters. His voice is needed. His message is powerful. And this book will change lives.

I'm proud to stand beside him.

**Lieutenant Kenny Mitchell Jr (Ret.)**,
Chesterfield, VA F.D., Founder: Operation Yellow Tape

# FOREWORD

In working together, Mike and I have become close friends. It is an honor to write this foreword for a man with the mission of using his pain as purpose to improve peoples' lives.

Mike's ability to get honest and authentic allows people to be authentic with him. In this book he dives into his life, both personal and professional. We are given a glimpse of how his formative years shaped him and many will identify with the challenges young Mike faced. The path Mike walked in those young years led him to a life of wanting to protect and help others.

The trials and tribulations in the daily life of a police officer are not things that many, including myself, are aware of. Mike recounts many events, both grave and humorous, and the sheer volume of the events is what struck me. Navigating daily life while experiencing powerfully painful moments, maintaining professionalism often requires the burying of emotion. Mike gets honest about the difficult moments and specifically how those seemingly dormant traumas breed chaos.

Progression is something many can identify with, destructive habits evolve and develop often in sinister ways. A little bit here, a little over there, soon becomes a lot everywhere. All who have made serious mistakes in life understand this and Mike does an incredible job at detailing this progression. Once harmless habits evolve into life changing decisions.

The pillars of importance that Mike lays out in conclusion are paramount. All will be better for focusing on the development of these areas. It requires an honest self-inventory and the shedding of fortified ego to sharpen and dial. Being real about where we are at and what areas need improvement allows us to finally cut the chains on those weights. We can't learn what we think we already know, we can't fix something that we don't know is broken.

Mike is solution oriented not problem focused. He leads with love and understands that his story is not just his to harbor but is to be shared for the raising of consciousness for all that are open to improve. Past traumas aren't a life sentence for a chaotic life. Mike demonstrates that traumatic events do not have to be an anchor but rather a catalyst for evolution and betterment. He lives by the philosophy that to know thyself better each day is the road to inner peace.

**Taylor Cavanaugh**, Former Navy SEAL
and French Foreign Legionnaire

# INTRODUCTION

I would like to thank you in advance for taking the time to read this book. As I began to write this in September 2025, I could not help but think that if ANYONE would've told ME that I would be writing a book approximately eighteen months ago, I would've laughed out loud and told them that they were absolutely nuts. I am a medically retired 30-year police officer and the last thing I believed that I would ever do is to write a book. Fortunately, MUCH has happened in my life during that time to change my perspective on both myself and life in general.

Eighteen months ago, I was a man who was not exactly what you would call "in touch with his emotions," to put it mildly. I look back to my childhood and when I TRULY examine it, what I deemed to be "normality" at the time, was actually a form of verbal abuse suffered at the hands of my father. He was an extremely stern guy, and I was a sensitive child so, to cope with the pain of feeling like a failure, or being called an "idiot" over and over and over, I began to callous up, to condition myself to not feel that pain. As a result, throughout the years, and especially after entering the law enforcement profession and trying to not absorb the pain that I saw all around me, I eventually taught myself to not feel ANYTHING, and that, is NO way to live life. In fact, that is not living at all. That is simply just existing, and that is a profoundly sad way to choose to spend this gift of life that we've all received.

This "journey" all began when I sat down in my backyard in Smithtown, NY, to watch a podcast episode of *The Shawn Ryan Show* sometime in the spring of 2023. Shawn was hosting a guest named Eddie Penney, a former Navy SEAL Team 6 Operator, and as I watched the episode, I had no idea that the ENTIRE trajectory of my life was about to change. Eddie began recounting the story of "The Extortion 17 incident," in which a Chinook transporting US Special Forces Operators was shot down by insurgents using an RPG on 8/06/2011 while in Afghanistan. Included in the dead were 38 service members, including 17 SEALs. It was their largest loss of life in one event in the entire history of their community. Included in the dead was Navy SEAL Jason Workman, Eddie's best friend, and as Eddie told the story of escorting Jason's body back home to his hometown, he was visibly upset, rightly so. I am a medically retired 30-year police officer veteran and as he spoke, I began thinking of a call that I had handled approximately five years before, that I had BURIED deeply involving a beautiful little two-year-old girl named Dana Sikorsky, who had been found floating in a pool. I realize now, that as Eddie cried, it subconsciously gave me permission to do the same, and I literally began crying like a baby. I was not sure what was going on as it was happening, but shortly thereafter I realized that I was suffering from some sort of PTSD. I had been retired for almost one year, and for about that length of time I had been experiencing bouts of depression, anger, rage, and general unhappiness, although I was unable to pinpoint the origins of these feelings. I always thought that PTSD was only suffered by seeing your brother or sister next to you get killed, but mine was caused by being inside the most devastatingly intimate moments of other people's lives over, and over, and over, and over, for 30 years. If you've never experienced the absolute most guttural, visceral cries that a human being can produce, I promise you two things: one, you never want to, and two, when you do, you will never EVER forget the sound that they make because it will make an indelible footprint on your soul for the rest of your life.

It was very shortly after this PTSD realization that I also realized that I needed help, and I knew that I did not want to be this ornery guy going through life hating everything and everyone.

I think it's important to go back to the beginning to examine what had gotten me to this point in life.

# THE RESILIENT WARRIOR

# CHAPTER 1

I was born in 1968 and was raised in N. Bellmore, NY, a suburb on Long Island, approximately 45 minutes east of Manhattan with my parents and younger sister. Growing up I believed that I had experienced a normal childhood. My father was a fireman for the FDNY, and my mom was a secretary for the local elementary school district in N. Bellmore. This afforded her weekends and summers off, so I always had pretty good supervision. I was a little bit of a wild kid but never got too out of control, knowing that my father "did not play." When it came to punishments, he was not shy about doling it out and between both of my parents, if there was some implement within arms-reach that could cause a little pain, that was what was going to be used!

The physical punishments were one thing, but I found myself the target of many divisive comments by my father throughout my childhood. I was a pretty sensitive kid, so they stung quite a bit. "What the hell do you know?", "Are you stupid?", "What the hell's wrong with you?", and "You are an asshole!" tended to add up after a while. I thought that this was absolutely normal, and knew no different or better, only that those comments hurt. At some point, I began callousing up, and saying not-too-nice things in my head to myself about my father in an attempt to deflect that pain.

I will speak about my usage of psychedelic therapies to heal from my traumas in later chapters, but after one particular journey with 5MeO-DMT (The God Molecule) in the spring of 2025, I was transported back to my house as an approximate eight-year-old and could remember the incident as though it had happened a minute before.

During the incident, I had just walked into my childhood home, and my father was hiding behind the front door. I laughed because I thought he was playing a game, but he was not. He walked up to me and PUNCHED me in the chest, knocking me off my feet clear across the room. As I was crying and attempting to catch my breath, I managed to utter the words, "Why did you hit me?" He told me he had done so because I was playing with a boy down the block that I was not supposed to ever play with. I struggled to speak but told him that I was NOT playing with the boy in question. The boy was speaking to another neighbor who I was actually playing with. I looked to my mother for help, but she stared at me with such disgust in her eyes that I've never forgotten that look to this very day!

To any parent who is reading this, I promise that incidents like this will NEVER be forgotten by your child, and I can CLEARLY remember thinking to myself at that time that I hated both of my parents.

Unfortunately, my father and I had never formed any kind of significant bond throughout my entire life, and looking back at my childhood now, with the years of life experience and perspective that I now hold, I think it is profoundly sad that my father was unwilling to let himself be vulnerable in any way, shape, or form, which would have allowed him to actually just TALK to me. This resulted in him never getting to know me and thus we never developed any bond whatsoever. Seriously think about that, and what an absolute shame it is that my father chose to forego a relationship with his only son because he could not figure out any way for us to bridge the gap since he was too prideful to ever just talk to me.

For those of you men who are reading this who have experienced something similar to what I did, I do not CARE how fierce you've become in your older years. You can literally be a Tier 1 war Fighter, a professional MMA Fighter, or anything else in between, if you do not heal from your childhood traumas, from things you believed that you never received in your formative years, things you probably NEVER will receive at this point, you STILL have to heal! These things don't just magically go away, they fester like an infection, and they will rear their ugly heads at the most inopportune times. If you are not processing, you're burying (compartmentalizing) or whatever terms you would like to describe your process, but I PROMISE you that these things will cause you to implode at some point.

I was always very good at athletics, and there was nothing that I loved more than playing sports when I was young. The criticism that I endured from my father about my athletic play was actually mind boggling. I remember one particular hockey game in which I had gotten credit for nine assists, and the entire car ride home my father lamented the fact that I did not score any goals. He actually became heated talking about how poorly I had played. I was in shock as I knew that I played a great game and apparently so did my coaches and the other parents because they were showering me with praise and were actually joking toward the end of the game about the next assist that I was about to receive.

I made a conscious decision during that car ride home. I STILL remember the exact intersection where we were stopped for a red light when I said to myself (excuse my language), "Fuck this guy! My teachers love me, my coaches love me, the parents of all of my friends love me, why doesn't this guy like me?" I vowed right then and there to let everything that he said go in one ear and out the other. I was no longer going to give significance to anything that he said to me.

Although I think it very sad that I had to make that vow to myself, it was all about self-preservation at that point, and I was not letting him, or anyone else in my life question my worth and create any self-esteem issues. I still think it miraculous to this day that I have never suffered any type of anxiety or low self-esteem disorder, because the foundation for that building was solidly in place!

# CHAPTER 2

As I progressed through my childhood and into high school, I believe that the relationship between my father and I essentially stayed the same. He NEVER spoke about work, and I mean, absolutely zero stories about anything that ever happened, so I'm sure that he never processed anything that he had seen. I specifically remember him being on the cover of a FDNY magazine called *With NY Firefighters*, (WNYF), and in one particular issue, the cover was a picture of him carrying two lifeless children out of the front door of a structure fire. Unfortunately, they had both perished in the fire, and I know that he had to have experienced a major trauma, but guys were told to just "suck it up" in those days. He never, ever spoke about work with me. I'm not sure if it was to shield me from the traumas that he had seen, but I have no context in which to put what he had experienced in his 36 years OTJ, "on the job."

Another instance of him and intense criticism occurred one day in the summer of 1986 when I came home after getting a flat-top haircut with my two friends, Rob Kenyon and John Warren, and upon walking in the front door, eager to show off my new "do," my dad stared at me and his initial remark was, "You look like an asshole." I was actually stunned but did not allow him the pleasure of knowing that fact and replied with, "You're really the best dad any guy could ask for," which I know stunned him as well.

I remember my father taking me to his firehouse on Myrtle Ave. in Ridgewood, Queens. He and his co-workers were known as "Myrtle Turtles" because apparently the firehouse was not the busiest in the city. On this particular day, when we walked into the firehouse, we were met by a firefighter that I had never met previously, and he made a comment to the effect of, "Your father never stops talking about you and your sports." I pointed to my own chest and asked, "Me?" He replied with a simple "yes," not really catching my drift and the fact that I was actually shocked. After much reflection and conversation with my wife over the past few years, I now realize that although he would never, ever give me praise, talking about my exploits in sports made him look good amongst the boys. It was a form of narcissism. It is actually quite sad that you search for an ulterior motive from your own father when he praises you for an accomplishment, but praise was never ever doled out, so I knew there was something else pushing that narrative.

I graduated from W.C. Mepham High School in Bellmore, NY, in 1986. I then went onto college, first attending Nassau Community College, then after graduating, went onto Hofstra University before graduating with a B.B.A. in accounting in May, 1991. Funny side note story, I played ice hockey at Hofstra Univ. and one of my teammates during the 1989-1990 season was none other than Jon Cooper, the current and multiple Stanley Cup winning coach of the Tampa Bay Lightning. If for some reason Coop gets this book in his hands, or if you're a friend of his, just say the word "Swingeeeeeer" really loudly and wait for his reaction. Unfortunately, that story cannot be told in the confines of this book!

Things stayed status quo between my father and me. They truly never really changed during the entirety of my life, sadly, but some things just aren't meant to be. After graduating from college, I was able to find a solid job in Manhattan working for Avon corporate as an Accountant. We were headquartered at "The 9 Building" on

W. 57th St. & 5th Ave, an absolutely beautiful part of Manhattan. A funny thing occurred on my first day of work though. It was sometime in mid-October 1991, and as I sat in my seat on the Long Island Railroad commuting into the city, I felt NOTHING. I was absolutely flat, which surprised me. Here I was on the first day of the rest of my life, embarking on this new career, and I should have been dripping with excitement, but I felt nothing, and really wasn't sure as to the reason why. After my arrival at work that morning, I was introduced to a boatload of associates, managers, partners, etc. At approximately 11:00 am, I was given a simple task and shortly thereafter I woke up with my head in my hand. I looked around quickly, praying that no one had seen this miscue, then got up, walked over to the cubicle of another associate whom I'd met earlier that morning and with whom I'd hit it off.

I asked him, "Do you like this stuff, bro?" His reply, which I'll never forget was, "Fuck no, I hate it!" I looked at him and said, "There is no way that I'm sitting in a cubicle for the next 30 to 35 years doing this. No one other than my close friends and family will even know that I lived, and I will make no impact whatsoever in this world!" I knew before lunch on my FIRST day of work in my new career that I was DONE. The question quickly became, "What do you want to do with your life?"

I pondered that question daily, actually all-day, every day. I had been training in martial arts with a now-mentor of mine, George Faherty, and although I've thanked him multiple times over the years, I'll do it here again.

"Thank you, brother. You changed my life in so many ways that I cannot even begin to tell you, and you UNDOUBTEDLY saved my life because you taught me how to become very proficient in very extreme violence."

I did not realize it at the time we began training, but it became clear throughout the years that George transformed me from someone who never looked for confrontation. When it occurred, I'd hope that it would get resolved quickly, and without me possibly having to get embarrassed in a fight, to someone who was EXTREMELY comfortable in any tense situation. And if my number was called, I had ZERO hesitation in answering that bell. In fact, I enjoyed it immensely. To me, the very essence of a man comes down to what he'll do when he's faced with a possible life or death situation, which can include fighting. I know what I've done as a man in those situations, and there's not even ONE time in which I was not proud of myself for the way that I had handled each and every one.

With this new found confidence, I believed that I was called upon to enter the field of law enforcement. It's difficult to explain to someone who's not had the calling, but I just felt that I had been molded into this man, by whatever higher power that you subscribe to, who could protect people from evil. I never had any disillusionment about being some superhero who was going to stop crime, only that I was going to do my little part to make the world a safer place to live.

The F.B.I. was my first choice as far as a desired position in law enforcement. I thought that "Special Agent Michael Morgan" had a nice ring to it. Unfortunately, the Universe had other plans for me as the entire federal law enforcement community was on a hiring freeze, which unbeknownst to me, would last until the late 1990s. The old adage, "When one door shuts, another one opens," was certainly true in my case as I met the brother (Rick) of a buddy of mine shortly thereafter. He had just relocated from NY to Atlanta after Pan Am airlines, his previous employer, had declared bankruptcy. Delta airlines had picked up his entire welding shop and offered jobs to him and all of his co-workers with a mandatory relocation to Atlanta.

Rick told me all about this great, vibrant, young city, and he really captured my attention. I had previously entertained thoughts of moving from NY, and Atlanta sounded like a great place for a young single guy to move to. I applied to the Atlanta Police Department shortly thereafter and began navigating the hiring process in the fall of 1992 before finally getting hired in August 1993.

I was extremely excited and scared at the same time, but it was time for me to begin living MY life! Unfortunately, my enthusiasm was not shared by my family, who were unhappy for several reasons. It began with my mother telling me, "You're leaving us!" The guilt that was heaped upon me in a concerted effort to get me to change my mind was incredible. My father, who literally NEVER, EVER talked TO me, just AT me, once again, never expressed any feelings to me upon hearing this news other than stating his extreme unhappiness with me leaving the prestigious accounting field for some "blue collar job." He'd always told my sister and I that his kids would NEVER take a civil service exam and that those jobs were for "peasants." I would always question him with, "So, that makes you a peasant?", but he would never reply to that particular question. My sister, who is actually one of the most despicable, disgusting human beings I've ever had the displeasure of knowing in my entire life, became an attorney—insert joke here— so at least one-half of his wish was realized.

I gave my two week-notice at AVON in mid-August 1993, packed up my life, got in my car, and drove down to Atlanta on August 21st 1993, ready to start my new life with zero support from my family.

# CHAPTER 3

I remember the 12-hour car ride to Atlanta on that Saturday 8/21/1993 (I drive quite fast) like it happened yesterday. There was no social media in 1993, cellphones themselves were in their early infancy, and I certainly did not have one. So, for the length of the trip, I listened to music on a cassette tape (kids will have no idea what I'm speaking about) that had been made for me by one of my lifelong friends, Mark Oster. I flipped it over as one side ended to listen to the other while I reflected deeply upon my life, and this major change that was unfolding right before my eyes. I remember feeling relief at "escaping" my parents' house, only realizing many years down the road how toxic the environment truly was living with my family. At that point, to me, it was just normal.

After arriving that night, I called home to let everyone know that I had gotten to Atlanta safely, and although my father spoke to me very briefly for the mandatory, "Glad you got there safe," I could hear the anger in his voice. My mother would not get on the phone with me; my sister told me, "Mommy's too upset to talk to you." I hadn't given it much thought at the time, but now, I consider that act, and many like it, to be self-serving and selfish. I was trying to live MY life, and my mother thought that it was selfish of ME to pursue MY dreams in the geographical location where I wanted to live. For anyone currently reading this book who is struggling in a similar situation, I promise that you will NOT make yourself happy living your life in ANY manner, or for someone else, other than the way that YOU would like to live it!

I was moving in with my buddy, the aforementioned Rick, who was away for the weekend, leaving me in the house solo, but I cannot express how deliriously happy I was to be living on my own and to be pursuing a career in what I now felt was my destiny.

I began working for the Atlanta Police Department on 8/24/1993 first as a recruit, since Atlanta would hire prospective police officers and farm them out to various details in the city until we had enough recruits to "class up." In my case, I worked for the Bureau of Taxis and Limousines until enough recruits were hired (34 in my class) to start an academy class at which time, we were all "transferred" into the Police Academy Command. My stint as a recruit was mostly uneventful, and I began the Atlanta Police Academy in early November of that year.

I came into the academy at the age of 25, 6'00" tall, weighing in at approximately 215-220 lbs. I was in very good physical shape. I know for the last P.T. (Physical Training) test, I was running a 6:04 mile, completed 93 push-ups, 140 sit-ups in 2 minutes, and did 19 pull ups. I could NOT do 20 in any of our P.T. tests, although I SHOULD have trained harder! I was definitely in the top percent of recruits performance-wise.

We concluded our academy training after 20 weeks but did not actually graduate until we had completed eight weeks of field training. On a Monday in mid-April 1994, I was given my first field training destination, the infamous Zone 3, who's moniker was "Little Vietnam," due to the amount of violence that occurred regularly in the confines of that precinct. Additionally, my first two weeks of field training were going to be on "Morning Watch," the dreaded 11:00 p.m.–7:00 a.m. tour!

Well, the following day came very quickly, and I still remember how excited I was that entire day; 11:00 p.m. could not come soon enough! My academy mate, Sam O'Neal, and I were graciously taken out for dinner that evening by his father prior to our first "tour." We were both assigned to Zone three morning watch our first two weeks, and I remember arriving at the precinct that night. The old Zone 3 precinct was located at 880 Cherokee Ave. (I did not even have to look that address up just now!), which backed up to the Atlanta Zoo. So, upon exiting my vehicle, I heard some crazy noises emanating from the zoo and that made me think, "You'd better get your mind right; you are literally entering a war zone!" Little did I know how right I was because only one hour into my first shift, with my Field Training Officer (FTO) Vic Franklin, I was brought to my first homicide scene. It was quite an interesting story actually; the homicide victim was a captain in the Atlanta Fire Department, who was on suspension from his job due to improper sexual allegations between him and underage girls.

On this night, they were absolutely confirmed when he decided to pick up a prostitute, in this case, a 16-year-old female. He then decided that he wanted to smoke crack while having sex. After getting the girl into his car, he drove up to the local dope boy (drug dealer) on the corner and when he "placed his order," the dope boy bent down, glanced in the car and who did he see? If you guessed that the dope boy saw his own 16-year-old cousin sitting in the passenger seat, then you would be correct! So, what would anyone do in that instance? If you guessed that the young drug dealer would pull out a gun and shoot the captain in the head, saturating the windshield with blood and brain matter, again, you would be correct!

It was a wild scene, and I distinctly remember thinking to myself, *some cops go their ENTIRE careers without seeing a homicide, and I've just done it an HOUR into my first tour.* The night was young however, I would soon realize. At approximately 4:00 a.m., we pulled into the empty parking lot of what was the Atlanta-Fulton County

Stadium to crack (take a nap). Vic reclined in his seat and was snoring about 30 seconds later. We worked five 8-hour days, and when you factor in the time that we worked "extra jobs," which were paid off-duty security details that were necessary because our salaries were disgustingly low, guys and girls were literal zombies, especially morning-watch cops. We know now how detrimental that bad/no sleep is for you, and when you factor in the other stressors that come with policing in an extremely violent city like Atlanta, it is no wonder that the burnout rate is so astronomically high. I literally had my head on a swivel as Vic napped for those approximate three minutes until the radio crackled with dispatch raising unit 1301 (us) for a call of a "50 & 4," which meant that we had just received a shooting call with an ambulance in route.

INCREDIBLY, before I could even say his name, Vic had woken up, pulled up his seat, hit the gas, grabbed the radio microphone, and acknowledged the call to the dispatcher. I was quite impressed to say the least, and as we headed toward danger, I was thinking, *this place is nuts*! Upon our arrival, we found a black male lying in the middle of the street at the intersection of Smith St. and Bass St. This was one of the only places that I was aware of in the precinct to purchase heroin, as opposed to crack or marijuana, which was never hard to find for those looking for it. People ridicule drug dealers as being stupid, but some are quite intelligent as you rise the ranks, and the organization that they employ in selling their wares can be quite impressive. As I looked down at this obviously newly deceased male, his eyes were wide open and appeared to be looking directly at me. I used to think to myself at every homicide scene that I went to, *Man, this guy was alive and doing his thing ten minutes ago.*

My academy buddy Sam O'Neal was at this second homicide scene with me, and as we looked at each other, I asked him, "What the fuck did we get ourselves into, bro?" A funny side story was that during this investigation, someone gave the homicide investigator (the rank of Detective did not exist at APD) the name of a possible perpetrator named "June Bug." A couple of months later while in the same general area, we received the nickname "June Bug" in relation to a possible drug dealer. I became excited, and I told my fellow officer, Kojo Joyner, that this person also was a possible suspect in a homicide investigation. As I explained to him why I believed this to be the case, he burst out laughing and told me that June Bug was a very common nickname in the black community. You learn something new every day as you go along in life, and that was my new nugget of knowledge.

# THE RESILIENT WARRIOR

# CHAPTER 4

T his introduction to life on the street was definitely an eye opener and an absolute harbinger of things to come, although it never gave me pause to reconsider my new career decision. In fact, I absolutely loved the action and the constant of knowing that anything could happen at any time.

Field training went very well, and we graduated shortly thereafter. At which time, I received my first assignment, to the ultra-violent Zone 3! I would like to say that things had gotten better with my family, but when I called them to provide the date of my police academy graduation in anticipation of them coming down to attend the ceremony, my mother simply said, "I'll talk to your father about it." I was stunned, but said nothing, believing they just wanted to express their unhappiness over my decision to leave New York and the accounting field. Unfortunately, she called back a few days later and said, "We can't make it."

I was at a loss for words and realized immediately that in many respects, I was on my own and would not be supported in any way in any issue in life if my parents disagreed with my decision. This proved to be prophetic in many ways, and from that point on, I always felt like the black sheep of the family. That wound and many others would never heal, but I was so emotionally repressed that I would/could never acknowledge the hurt and disappointment. Instead, I used anger to fuel me in many respects, and as many of us know, that is not a healthy way to manage your emotions.

For the next year, I was assigned to the mini precinct located on Stewart Ave, which has since been renamed Metropolitan Pkwy for the absurd reason that Stewart Ave, which was known far and wide as a place filled with seedy hotels, strip clubs, prostitutes, drug dealers etc., would somehow be seen in a more favorable light if it was renamed. This is how government works. One person comes up with the absolute dumbest idea you've ever heard in your life, and you think to yourself that no one will take it seriously. The next thing you know, as it was in this case, new street signs are being erected days later after hearing the proposal for the first time. I hate to sound negative, but I would bet quite a bit of money that there was some sort of corruption influencing this sort of decision.

While at mini precinct, I worked with approximately ten other officers, and we walked a foot beat for the next year. We got into so many crime investigations including drug dealing, stolen cars, and prostitution that our own Sgt. Dale Hendrix commented that he'd never seen foot beat cops get into so much in his entire career. Ironic side note, Hendrix was arrested for corruption sometime in 1995. Most of us had to testify at his trial. Somehow, he beat the charge, which none of us could ever figure out, because we all thought he was guilty as sin!

I loved what I had chosen as career path and looked forward to going to work every single day.

I remember one particular night, my partner, Jose Vidal (R.I.P., Brother) and I were asked by two investigators who worked for the F.I.T. Team (Field Investigations Team), which was essentially a street crimes unit, if we'd like to go out with them in plainclothes. To say we were pumped was the understatement of the year and as we changed into our "civvies," I said to Jose, "I wonder what we're gonna get into, bro." It did not take long to find out.

We began driving around and were looking for anything unusual, which is what you do as a police officer. At approximately 8:00

p.m., we turned onto a certain street in the "Pittsburgh" section of Southwest Atlanta to investigate several spots of known drug dealing. We stopped at one and began speaking to several gentlemen who were just "chillin." The investigators that we were with, Entrikin and Harrington, were well known to everyone in the area, especially Harrington, who was known as "Reebok" because he wore white high-top Reeboks every single day.

We ended up kind of surrounded (nothing adversarial, things just unfolded that way) by the guys we were speaking with. This led to the occupants of a Jeep that had just pulled up in front of the group not realizing that police officers were in their midst. We quickly walked towards the Jeep that had now stopped at the curb, and I shined my flashlight into the car. I immediately was drawn to the butt of a gun sticking out of the right pocket of the Carhart jacket the passenger was wearing. I quickly opened the door, removed the gun from the pocket of the passenger, now known to me as "Ric-Ric" and put it in my rear pocket. I mistakenly told the passenger to get out of the car and put his hands behind his back, instead of immediately grabbing his wrist and forcing him down to the ground. As he exited the vehicle, my partner got between us, and when I told Ric-Ric to place his hands behind his back, he instead elbowed Jose in the face and took off running with me close behind. I gave chase, and he attempted to make a right turn but slipped and fell on the gravel. When he scrambled to his feet, he squared off with me. It is interesting because the first time or two that you're required to use physical force at work on a subject, you're unsure of the amount to use. By law, it is the amount of force that is just greater than the force they're employing against you to overcome their force, but in practice, at first, you're not truly sure where that line is.

I got in a fighting stance myself, and he threw a left jab at me which I blocked (just as I was taught by George!) downward with my right hand. I still had my flashlight in my left hand and struck his left collarbone in an attempt to break it, but I went a little too high. I missed my mark, but he screamed out in pain, grabbed his left shoulder which left him wide open for me to grab the back of his head in a Muay Thai clench, and pulled his head quickly down to my right knee which met his face rather violently. I popped that grape (nose) wide open. In that instant, unbeknownst to me, I created a very solid reputation for myself on the street as I unknowingly just whooped the ass of the biggest drug dealer in the area. He was the big dog.

I found out in later years that he was essentially a serial killer, although no one would testify against him due to the well-founded fear that he would get them too. A funny addendum to that story was that I had received a notification for a federal parole revocation hearing in court because Ric-Ric was on federal probation and the gun charge triggered a revocation.

During that hearing, I was testifying when one of the attorneys asked for side bar with the judge, who was seated to my left. As they all spoke in front of the judge, I began looking around the room and ended up locking eyes with the defendant. We began intently staring at each other, and I meant to MOUTH the words, but actually said out loud, "Fuck You!" I don't know how that judge did not get whiplash because her head slammed to the right faster than I don't know what! I glanced at the prosecutor, who probably didn't know whether to shit or go blind and her mouth was wide open. I would've loved to have captured the entire thing on tape for posterity's sake.

We were transferred as a group to the mobile precinct in May 1995, and the action only got better from there.

# CHAPTER 5

After getting transferred to the "big" precinct, we were assigned to patrol cars and were charged with handling 911 calls on evening watch, 3:30-11:30 p.m., and it was the trip of a lifetime. I had become very familiar with what we were going to be tasked with handling after my year of foot beat policing, but being in patrol cars and actually handling these calls was a different animal altogether. The sheer volume of calls was incredible, and in the warmer months, it was quite normal to be handling 30 or more calls every single night. July 1995 was an incredibly violent month. In fact, if I remember correctly, that month Atlanta recorded 37 homicides, which was the deadliest month ever in their history. I was called to quadruple back-to-back-to-back-to-back shootings one particular night, and another night that summer had us going to triple back-to-back-to-back shootings. I will guarantee that there are few cops ever, who can say that.

My cousin Tim had come down to visit one week, and he came to work with me and did a ride-a-long. He retired from the NYPD with the rank of captain after a 29-year career, but at the time, he was a police officer on patrol in the "8-3", east New York (a very tough part of New York City) with approximately nine years OTJ (on the job). We were about two hours into my tour when he looked at me and said, "Morgs, you gotta get the FUCK outta here!"

I asked, "Why?"

"This is insanity," he replied. "This makes the "8-3" look like a country club. You guys don't even have partners." He was absolutely right, it was insanity, but I loved every minute of it at that time.

The two biggest things I hunted for were drugs and stolen cars. And when you're looking for those two things, you are inevitably also going to find guns, violence, and pursuits. I could not begin to estimate how many car/foot pursuits that I was involved in in Atlanta, both those started by me and those in which I was a responding unit to other officer's calls. As I stated before, I loved the action. Only those who've done it can understand, but there is NOTHING like hunting another man, especially an evil one. That adrenaline rush cannot be duplicated by anything else that I've experienced in life, and I felt like I was put on this earth to do that job.

Unfortunately, with all that action comes some sobering things that happen all around you. You see death and destruction on a scale that was unimaginable to you prior to gaining a front row seat to the greatest show on earth. How to healthily process these things that you see and can never unsee, so that they lose their "emotional charge" and power over you is one of the most valuable things you could possibly bring to this job. Unfortunately, I did not realize this during the entirety of my career, and it would come back to haunt me.

The first "traumatic" call that I can remember handling came in the early spring of 1996. Although I had already handled homicides, suicides, fatal motor vehicle accidents, and natural deaths, this call stuck with me for quite a while, even after I had compartmentalized (BURIED) it. I had received a call of an aided case, which is a medical call, involving an 11-year-old non-responsive male. Upon my arrival, I heard screaming coming from within even before I knocked on the door. After entering the apartment, I entered the living room to find a young black male lying on the floor, looking up at the ceiling. Three grown women were also in the room, in hysterics, and I would later be told that they were his mother, grandmother, and aunt, respectively. I bent down to see if he had a pulse, but he was ice cold, and there nothing that anyone could've done for him at that point. However, I decided that there was no way that I was going to just stand there with my thumb up my ass while these three women were making the most visceral heartbreaking sounds that any of you who are reading this can pray that you never have to hear yourselves.

I radioed my dispatcher and told her to "step up" rescue and stated that CPR was in progress. I performed CPR, which for those who've ever done it know, is exhausting. Performing it solo, with three screaming women behind you, knowing the child you're performing it on is irretrievably dead cannot be explained in words. It is just someplace that you NEVER want to be.

A very strange thing was happening as I was doing compressions on the boy; I heard liquid coming up his airway and although my medical training was very limited at that point in time, I knew that it should not be happening. I turned the boy on his side to expel the liquid that sounded like it was about to bubble up into his mouth, and green liquid poured out of him. FD and rescue walked through the door at that moment, and I just looked up at them and mouthed the words, "What the fuck?" Thank God they decided to scoop the boy up and transport him to the hospital or else I would've had to spend hours at the apartment waiting for homicide and crime scene to come out and process the scene with these poor women by my side.

En route to the hospital I was tasked with transporting one of the females, I believe it was the child's aunt, and she just kept repeating the phrase, "Please tell me he's going to be all right, officer." I knew good and well that there was no hope whatsoever, but I just kept telling her (and for those of you who are still active officers, NEVER promise something that is untrue. In this case, that would have been me telling her that "he's going to be fine"), "They are doing everything that they can, ma'am."

After we arrived at the hospital, doctors took me and the rescue units into a room to inform us that the boy had died of bacterial meningitis. They also said that it was rarely transmitted from children to adults but to be on the safe side they were going to give me a massive dose of antibiotics and told me to self-quarantine for the next 48 hours. I remember driving back to the precinct and thinking to myself that had I not been told to quarantine myself, I would be going right back into service without speaking to anyone about anything that I had just witnessed. As it turned out, I was never asked by anyone if I was okay after that call, no co-workers, no bosses, no one.

Things like that usually weren't discussed by anyone back "in the day." After leaving work, I walked over to Ansley Park, a huge park in Atlanta, and just sat on a small hill unable to think about anything other than that child and those three women whose lives were NEVER going to be the same, and it happened right before my eyes.

# CHAPTER 6

Amidst doing the job that I loved, there were things I had experienced, and things that I was currently experiencing, that gave me pause for reflection. I was blown away by the amount of hate that was thrown our way as police officers. The first time I heard the term, "White Devil," I was actually shocked. I had taken this job to protect people from evil and do my little part to help society, but being hated because of the uniform that I wore definitely took some getting used to. We would go into the housing projects, and many times, babies and children would smile, wave, and say, "Hi, police," only for their hand to be slapped down by their mother who told them, "Don't you ever talk to the police!"

It was a very strange dynamic, and I obviously wasn't naïve. I knew there was a difficult history between some minority groups and the police, but until it's said directly to you, you don't realize that it's a quite a hurtful statement. I always wanted to scream back, "This isn't my neighborhood that I'm willing to sacrifice my life for. I'm here to help you," but I wasn't going to change the minds of people who were filled with that level of hatred, with words.

To me, a subject that was of utmost importance was physical training, both in fighting, and in pumping iron at the gym. I knew that it was not a question of if, but when, your number was going to get called, causing you to be in a potentially life-or-death situation. Obviously not everyone that I worked with felt the same way, and I could NEVER reconcile the fact that officers did not prepare for the inevitable. I saw men and women who were fearful to perform their job on a daily basis, and I could not imagine the stress that they put themselves under, living in constant fear of "what if." One of the things I most loved about the job was that you never knew what was going to happen minute-to-minute, but that same thought instilled incredible fear in some people, and to me, they experienced PTSD almost daily. This because they were too lazy to prepare themselves for battle, and make no mistake about it, we went to battle every day. Some days you got lucky, and there was no battle to be fought, other days though, showed how just how fragile life was.

I could not imagine going to work every day praying that things would go smoothly because I was incapable of handling the evil that was being brought to me! I remember one specific instance of this being illustrated perfectly when one day a call came over the radio in my sector while I was handling a car accident on I75-85. The call was regarding a domestic, and the narrative was that a women's son was being violent and flipping out on both her and her sister (both in their 70's). Another cop in my precinct that rode a mini motor (small motorcycle) copied the call (said that he would handle the call), although he was a guy that had ZERO business going to a call like that alone. I had just finished handling the accident, told dispatch that I was en route to it, and then told the other unit to meet me at a specific intersection whereupon we would arrive together. He stated "affirmative" but decided to then mistakenly approach the house alone, at which time I told him to wait, knowing that he couldn't handle a lost cat call on his own, let alone this, but he disregarded that message and again approached alone. There is NOTHING scarier than a guy trying to prove himself on the streets, especially when he's got zero bona-fides to actually do so! Seconds later, a burglary detective that worked in our precinct began transmitting over the radio, essentially stating that the unit on scene was getting his ass kicked, that the perpetrator had body slammed him and had removed his gun belt from his person. This ramped up the seriousness of the call 1,000 times due to the perpetrator now having a fully functional .9mm Glock if he was able to figure out how to remove the gun from the Level III Retention holster that we wore.

I arrived on scene to find the officer quite shaken and disheveled, along with our Lieutenant (Lt.), the watch commander for day tour, which I was now assigned to since the spring of 1996. The Lt. was apprised of the situation, then turned to me and said, "Go get him," knowing full well that I loved being in the middle of the craziness. I simply asked him, "I got the green light?" To which he replied, "Absolutely." I could not contain my smile knowing that I was about to get into some serious shit and had ZERO intention of coming back as anything but the victor!

I walked up to the front door with my buddy, McCrary, and his recruit who was in field training after having just left the academy. His recruit's first name was Major, and I loved that name. Plus, he was a monster and did not seem to be afraid of the possible danger that awaited us. I knocked one time on the front door then turned around and horse kicked it right off its hinges, which got me really pumped up! Then I just kind of yelled out, "You-Hooooo," but we received no answer, so I yelled for him to come out, or he was not going to be a happy guy. He peeked around a corner and said, "I didn't do nothin," a common refrain from my Zone 3 days. We walked to him in a very tactically sound manner and upon entering his room, he stood up quickly, (had nothing in his hands), and charged me at which time I struck him across the very top of his chest, just under his throat as I held my nightstick with both hands, knocking him completely off of his feet onto his back, and as he attempted to catch his breath, he was quickly cuffed. We brought him outside, and my Lt. who appeared stunned said, "How did you do it that fast?" I just laughed and said, "Major did it."

I looked at the original officer and thought to myself, that dude's going to get someone killed one day, and I was right, but it was me that he almost got killed, but that story will have to wait for my next book! Unfortunately, this officer learned nothing from that incident as he neither began to lift weights or learn how to fight. But he did look really, really cool as he smoked his Marlboro reds. To those who are reading this book with the anticipation of becoming a police officer, or for those who are currently active duty, train your ass off and you will be ready for most anything that can come your way, and you will also never have to live with that daily stress that not being prepared will surely bring you.

To further illustrate the stress of the job and the potential of things to accelerate from 0-100 in seconds, I'd like to highlight a call that my partner and I encountered that nearly cost us our lives. I was operating unit 3304 with Frank Lupo, a great guy, great cop, and great friend on a weeknight as we worked a 3:30-11:30 p.m. tour in July '95. The odd numbered patrol units started work 30 minutes earlier than the even numbered cars and were also called into the precinct 30 minutes earlier than the late cars at the end of our tour. On this night, the supervisor had called in the early cars when we received a call of a fight with a possible gun involved in Thomasville Heights, one of THE most violent housing projects in all of Atlanta, which sat just down the block from the Atlanta Federal Penitentiary. We were on the other side of the precinct when we received the call, and it was a hike to get there so we proceeded that way. As we drove, we received additional updates from our dispatcher. She had stated that the perpetrator had gotten into a physical altercation with the brother of his girlfriend, and the brother had beat him up handily. The perpetrator then threatened to shoot the brother and left the location to "get his gun." It took us approximately fifteen minutes to get to the scene, and as we pulled up to the side of the building, we saw a Black male point a handgun into an apartment and start shooting.

We advised dispatch we had "25's on-call" (shots fired) and exited the patrol car as the perpetrator ran around the side of the building towards the back of it, when he spotted us. He then turned left to run behind the building but quickly turned around and began firing directly at us. We had someone speak to us during my time as a recruit in the Atlanta police academy regarding the physiological effects experienced by the body during high-stress situations, which include a muted auditory response (you don't hear well) as well as tunnel vision. True to form, as he was firing his .357 revolver at us, I did not hear the gun fire. I only saw the muzzle flashes, and as I looked at the perp, it was absolutely tunnel vision that I was experiencing. I felt relatively calm though and a voice inside my head simply said, "Kill him." Unfortunately, the back stop was not clear as there were a bunch of people standing behind him on that hot July night so neither of us was able to return fire. We lost him fairly quickly but could hear the troops coming to assist us at a distance.

We were canvassing the area when we received a call approximately ten minutes later of a possible burglary at an apartment in that immediate area. Four of us (the two that had joined us, PO's Sauls, and Pinckney were EXACTLY two of the officers we would've chosen to back us up!) approached the apartment, found a broken front door, and began searching the premises. We cleared the first floor then crested the stairs as we went to search the second floor. I opened the door slightly as the other three officers walked to my right, peeked in to see that no one was standing behind it, then looked into the room and saw an approximately two-year-old boy sitting upright in bed, wide awake at 11:30 p.m., which I thought strange. I whispered, "Hey, buddy, is anyone else in here with you?" and he nodded. I then asked, "Where is he?", to which he pointed at his empty crib. I then made a "pssst" sound to my co-workers, and whispered, "He's under the crib to the right," and we kicked the door open, turned the lights on, flipped the crib over, and found our man, who decided he was going to fight his way out of that situation. It did not go well for him though, and he was placed into custody, wherein the boy's father came into the room and got the child, who was unharmed. I told the child that he had done a great job and asked him if the man had anything with him when he entered the room, to which he nodded. I asked him where he had put it and he pointed to the mattress which I immediately picked up and found his .357 revolver, which had once again been fully RELOADED! I did my usual AAR (After Action Report) and was happy with how we had all handled the situation, but the adrenaline dumps that we experienced on those extremely dynamic and dangerous calls were incredible, and I knew in my heart that they were not exactly advantageous for our nervous system!

# CHAPTER 7

The 1996 summer Olympics were held in Atlanta, and my summer was mostly uneventful except for the sheer workload. We literally had our names picked from a hat to decide whether we were going to be assigned to the Olympic detail or stay in the Zone and continue to perform patrol duties. The concept of "Be careful what you wish for" was illustrated perfectly here as I was quite happy that I had gotten chosen to stay in the precinct, but after 3 ½ weeks of handling 30-plus calls on a 6 days on/1 day off schedule with twelve-hour tours, I was experiencing quite a bit of burnout. I still had to go to work every day with my head "in the game," because evil lurked everywhere and was not taking a break for the Olympics.

On one particular morning, I remember driving around my "beat" immediately after 7:00 a.m. roll call, and as I proceeded south on Stewart Avenue from Ralph David Abernathy Blvd, I heard gunshots ring out. I transmitted over the radio to dispatch that "I hear 25's (gunshots) in the area" and was driving quite slowly when to my left, I observed a young Black male coming out of the bushes in front of a house across the street from my location, holding a gun in his right hand. I immediately threw my gear shift into park, jumped out of my patrol car, drew my gun down on the subject (who I immediately realized was a guy named Al, whom I'd previously arrested for possessing a large amount of crack), and shouted for him to "drop the gun!" Al took his time putting that gun on the ground, and I was ready to begin shooting if he made any sudden movements as I had my sights aimed squarely on his chest. He decided that he did not want to escalate the situation and dropped the gun to the ground. at which point, I was able to get him handcuffed and into custody. Al once again was discovered to be in possession of a large amount of crack that was in a plastic bag and had been secreted in one of his socks. He explained to me that the two gunshots that I had heard were fired from an unknown perpetrator as he attempted to rob Al in his backyard.

It was probably not even 8:00 a.m., less than an hour into my tour, and I was almost already involved in an officer-involved shooting. I always conducted "after action reports" regarding my tactical response and readiness in various situations, and in most cases, I did rather well since I always took my job and training very serious. I realized the importance of always staying focused, even though ALL is an impossible standard to achieve. It was extremely hard to focus on the job at hand continuously because of the different things occurring in my personal life, but you had to learn to tune them out or face serious consequences for becoming distracted.

In some respects, you were almost fighting a battle on two fronts in that you experience the different traumas and battles of everyday life, then you go to work for eight hours, and have THOSE traumas and battles heaped upon you. There are so many lessons that I've learned over the years regarding the importance of, and the process of, releasing those traumas, but truth be told, I would never allow myself to become vulnerable enough to process those traumas anyway during my career. In my mind, it was weakness to even acknowledge the fact that something had affected me negatively, and if you don't acknowledge it, there's no way in the world that you're going to be able to heal from that pain.

# CHAPTER 8

I remained on patrol until I received a requested transfer to the Motorcycle Squad in June 1998. I had mixed feelings about leaving the zone. I was definitely going to miss many of my co-workers, but I was also very excited to go to this new detail which offered much more freedom and a better quality of life. Additionally, our salaries were so ridiculously low that, as mentioned earlier, you were forced to work EJ's (Extra Jobs) to supplement your income. It was well-known that the officers on the motorcycle squad were privy to some of the best paying EJ's that existed. Unfortunately, one thing I was not counting on was having to now work under a sergeant who was undoubtedly the single biggest piece of garbage that I would encounter in my entire 30-year career.

As I got more experience, and saw this clown in action, I asked myself a million times how he got away with treating his subordinates so poorly. I'll give him this: although he wasn't the smartest of people, he knew who to take care of. He ran two of the highest paying EJ's in the department. One was for a running club organization that held road races all around Atlanta throughout the year and the other for a big amphitheater in Atlanta. He would give the majors (We used Military rank structure, a major was one step above a captain) and, I believe, deputy chiefs great assignments on both of those jobs. These bosses would spend as little time as possible at the detail but received the full monetary benefit as the rest of us who were made to stay for the entirety of the event. This made him untouchable with the brass, even though he had ZERO ability to either lead or inspire anyone to do anything.

I mention him specifically because I think it's important to illustrate the fact that some of THE most intense stress that we'll ever encounter comes from within our own organization. It's truly incredible to me that there are bosses out there who are so power hungry that they not only dismiss the stressors facing the troops under them, but they also saddle them with even more. I've seen as many men/women leave the police department because of the negativity that they experienced internally, as externally! Between nepotism and downright incompetence, these two things can destroy the morale of a police department and cause immeasurable harm to the culture within. It truly takes only one bad apple to destroy, rather quickly, what in some cases took years to build. I am as straight-a-shooter as you will find, and I had actually asked this boss TWICE during my time there if he'd like to discuss things outside, man to man, and true to form, being the coward that he was, the offer was declined. I'm not saying that I was correct in asking a fellow employee to decide an issue using physical violence, but to me, it was the purest, most honest way to squash a beef. There were two distinct camps regarding this supervisor. You had a few guys that liked him because he kept them employed with great EJ's, and the rest of the squad, who refused to work for him, and who actually hated him.

I remember feeling burnout while on motors periodically solely because I hated working for this man so much, and even my then-Lt. would make jokes at the Sgt's expense regarding his "leadership ability," knowing that he had none, but was untouchable. He was even given a nickname, "The Golden Boy." It was a moniker that fit him well.

For those of you who find yourself in this situation, my advice would be to try and get along with him/her. There is CONSTANT change in the police department, and their assignment is probably temporary. If, however, it truly begins to affect you, look for another detail. The stress that you're experiencing is not good for your mental health, and it will begin creeping into every facet of your life, if you let it do so.

To those current supervisors who may be reading this book, or those who may become supervisors in the future, you will have absolute potential to influence the quality of life that the men and women who serve under you experience. Instead of trying to "flex" on them and prove to them that you are the one in charge, as a weak-minded individual is apt to do, realize that the troops will run through walls for supervisors that they respect, and who respect them. Counter that with those supervisors who attempt to lead by fear or intimidation. Those troops will do the absolute bare minimum, will hop on any opportunity to make you look bad, and can never truly be trusted by that supervisor, as they have no vested interest in helping them shine. I was in this field for thirty years and to this day, I cannot understand how supervisors do not realize that if they do not respect the troops, the troops will never respect them.

A supervisor who attempts to relieve stress from their subordinates, as opposed to heaping it onto them, will garner the same efforts from the troops a thousand times over! That one rotten supervisor, who could've helped the squad be extremely tight, instead was responsible for so much bitterness, stress, and divisiveness.

I remember, shortly after being transferred to motors, that I had the opportunity to purchase a Honda Valkyrie from the officer who's place I had just taken when he got transferred to the Mounted Patrol section. There was a company that paid you to do motorcycle escorts for funerals, wherein you would escort the procession from the church, or funeral home, to the cemetery, but you had to use your personal motor to do so. This officer reached out and offered to sell me his bike, a Honda Valkyrie for $6K. It was a great deal, a mechanic pronounced it to be in great condition, and I called my father to see if he would loan me the money. I proposed a $6K loan with a six-month payment term, and the monthly minimum payback would be $1K so I would pay my father $7K in total, including $1K in interest. My father replied with, "I'll think about it," which definitely took me back as I've had two jobs since the age of 12, had paid for my entire college education, started paying rent IMMEDIATELY after my college graduation, and had paid my father back for another car loan that he'd given me in 1992, in its entirety.

In other words, I was not a risk. I've always paid back any monies I've EVER owed, in its entirety, and on time. You can imagine my amazement when a few days later, my father informed me that he "would not feel comfortable loaning me the money." I was in shock and questioned his reasoning. He told me that the previous loan given to me in 1992 was paid back late, causing me to pause momentarily, then I replied that "Yes, when I left Avon and started with Atlanta, there was a six-week lag in paychecks so I asked you if I could skip that month then resume payments the following month," which he had agreed to, and I continued doing so until it was paid in its entirety, one month late. He again responded that he did not feel comfortable giving me the money (unknown to me at the time was that my parents had a few hundred thousand dollars in the bank, so although I would NEVER, EVER not repay it, if I had chosen that route, they would not be destitute), and he would not be doing so. I responded with, "Fine. Don't worry. I'll never ask you for anything else the rest of my life," and did not.

The craziest part of this story is that shortly after speaking to my father, I told this story to one of my new buddies on the motors squad, Tim McEwing, whom I'd known all of two months, more because I was in shock than anything else. Tim simply responded with, "I'll have a check for you tomorrow." I was stunned and replied that I was not asking him for the money. I was simply telling him this story. He stated that he knew I wasn't, which is why he was giving it to me. Tim was also a personal injury attorney on the side so he did well financially, but in no way, shape, or form did he have to do that for me. It was incredible. My own FATHER said he would not help me yet, but this guy that I hardly knew agreed to do so!

As promised, the loan terms were honored, and Tim had received his $7K in six months. Sadly though, I had little love in my heart for my father ever again. I had thought at the time that he thought so little of me that he wouldn't even lend me money. Now though, after much introspection, I realize, after my wife had pointed it out to me over the past couple of years that that he had said no as a form of control, he did not agree with my decision to leave NY, or become a police officer, and certainly did not want me to become a motorcycle officer. Unfortunately, he had hurt me DEEPLY in that incident, although I was unable to express that to him emotionally at the time.

I lay my heart bare for all of you men (women are quite different at expressing emotion, as we all know) to show you the importance of allowing yourselves to become vulnerable. If I had possessed a higher emotional intelligence at the time, perhaps I could've salvaged our relationship somehow, but I was totally unaware and incapable of expressing feelings to my father. I found out many years later that he had confided to other people that he did not know why I held so much anger towards him, that he hadn't done anything wrong. But, of course, he could never approach me with that question himself because that would've made him vulnerable. I'm certainly not suggesting that everything I've ever done or said was correct, but he never even tried to meet me halfway, and if I'm being honest, I always TRIED to be the good son, but I should have excised my father from my life a very long time ago. His energy and personality were so negative and caustic and brought me zero happiness whatsoever.

It would have been incredibly difficult to do though, because this would've meant the loss of my mother, and who knows how many other family members, because no one had any idea how toxic he was. He showed the outside world one side of him but hid the other, for the most part. Even towards his own brother, he had a noticeable change in demeanor the second he would encounter him, with one-word answers and just an absolutely negative energy. I would ask him throughout the years, "What's with you and Uncle Gerry?" The overwhelming number of times he would not answer me, but twice he replied with, "He's an asshole," and nothing more. Meanwhile my Uncle Gerry was THE nicest guy going, and though he was relatively strict with his children, he did not have that sharp, biting personality that cut people down that my father did. My father was an absolutely NASTY man a fair amount of the time.

I had returned back to New York from Atlanta one time for a week-long visit after living there for approximately five years and on the car ride home from the airport, I had asked my father, "When are you guys going to come to Atlanta?" His nasty reply was, "What the hell would I want to go to Atlanta for?" My first thought was, "This guy's my FATHER?" I then replied with, "Because your son lives there." He did not respond, but that literally illustrates our loving relationship in a nutshell. It was not something that I ever discussed with anybody because I was so embarrassed at the things that he said to me and—this is insane—I was afraid that if I told anyone what he said and did on the regular that they would dislike him! Is that insane that he was so verbally abusive, yet I was worried about people looking at him in a negative light if I ever told them the truth about our relationship.

# CHAPTER 9

Things were status quo for a while at work. Motors was fine and bosses rotated in and out on a semi-regular basis, so you were excited to work for some bosses, and others, not so much. I had gotten back into playing ice hockey in early 2001 after many years of not doing so, and I decided that I wanted to start an Atlanta Police hockey team and put some feelers out but quickly realized that we were not going to be able to field a full team using just the Atlanta PD, so I decided to include the Atlanta Fire Department as well. Unfortunately, I still did not have the numbers I was going to need—we were in the deep south after all—so I decided to open it up a little more and finally named it, The Metro Atlanta PD/FD Hockey Team, wherein I was able to attract enough guys to field a team.

We were scheduled to begin practice the second week of September 2001, but we all know what happened on 9/11/01, which pushed back the date of our first practice to mid-November 2001. Interestingly enough, my ex-wife and I had been in NY for vacation and were scheduled to fly out on 9/10/01, but there were bad thunderstorms in New York that night which delayed our departure until 12:30 a.m. on 9/11/01. We awoke the next morning to my phone ringing incessantly, and after answering it, was told by my father to put the television on, where we watched the second plane strike the World Trade Center. When the buildings fell, I distinctly remember looking at my wife and saying, "Do you know how many cops and firemen just died?"

Shortly thereafter, I received a call from my command telling me to report to the precinct at our usual tour time, 3:30 p.m. At which, we were all informed that we would be working at Hartsfield Airport for the foreseeable future. It was VERY eerie pulling up to the airport, the WORLD's busiest, although it was almost empty as our squad rolled up with approximately 30 motorcycles in total. We were given assignments, mine being inside one of the terminals, along with my NEVER boring buddy and police academy-mate, Carl Juhls. I guarantee that ANYONE who knows both of us just made a face when they read that last sentence because Juhls and I together spells "funny shit's about to happen" time! We were not in the most jovial moods at this time, however. Along with millions of others, I was heartbroken, but certainly also filled with rage and a huge dose of survivor's guilt which kicked in surprisingly quickly after the towers fell.

I remember sitting in the empty terminal that night. There were no airplanes departing or arriving, and there was LITERALLY no one around, period. It felt like we were in an episode of an apocalyptic movie, but you were unable to change the channel, and I kept thinking that life was never going to be the same again. I also seriously contemplated joining the military to be one of the ones to deliver the payback that those terrorists so richly deserved. Those thoughts were quelled rather quickly when I thought about my age, 33, and how long it would take to get me trained up and "in the fight."

I ended up getting assigned outside the terminals with my buddy Kenny Stapler (Stape) for the remaining week that we spent at the airport, which we both loved because we hated being inside. I remember that one night we were told a medi-flight was going to depart with an organ being transported somewhere for a transplant. It was INCREDIBLY strange to hear that one flight depart, and I was eventually able to see that ONE plane in the sky—nothing but stars and that one plane—as all commercial flights were still grounded.

Here's another example of horrendous leadership, and its effect on employee morale. We ended up working overnight tours at the airport for a week, and we were tasked with setting up a semi-checkpoint for vehicles that were going to be parking next to the police precinct in a small lot. Only high-level personnel knew about this spot as the airport was still closed, so we set up a traffic cone slightly offset, and this essentially showed the entrance to be closed, but those who had parked there for the last two nights realized they had enough room to drive past it and into the parking lot.

At approximately 6:30 am, a motorcycle squad day-tour sergeant came pulling up in his little red Mercedes two-door and stopped. This particular guy and I had always gotten along, although he is probably one of THE most arrogant people I've ever met in my ENTIRE life (though I have no idea why), and he was immensely disliked by a large portion of the guys in the squad. I looked at Stape and said, "Watch this tool say some dumb shit right here", and true to form, he begins to beep his horn. I was about 30 feet away and motioned for him to drive around it, but he hit his horn again and pointed at the cone. I'll remind anyone reading this book that he was driving a very compact two-seater that EASILY could've driven by the traffic cone. I then walked up, picked the cone up and he drove by me, parking about 100 ft away, close to the terminal. I watched as he exited his car and put his gun belt on while looking back towards Stape and me. I told Stape, "It's killing him, bro. There is NO way he's going inside without saying something to me."

He then called for me to come over to him, and I started walking as slowly as was humanly possible because I was not in the mood for this condescending fool. 9-11 was just a couple of days old at this point, we were all wrecked emotionally, and this so-called "leader" was now going to try and flex on me to prove that he was "El Jefe" regarding the placement of a traffic cone! He then launches into this soliloquy about it being my job to move the cone for anyone, but I definitely should've moved it when I saw

HIM approach the entrance, etc., etc. As I listened to this narcissist speak, I was getting madder by the second.

First off, any leader worth his salt would've driven by the cone, rolled down his window, and asked Stape and I how we were doing, as did almost every person that had passed us prior to entering the lot. Almost every other person that had driven passed us was a high-level "fed" who didn't know either of us yet, they all had the common decency and respect to say hello, and at least feign interest as to our well-being.

Normally, I am extremely respectful to supervisors, I live by the adage, "If you don't respect the man, respect the rank," but I could not help myself. As he began to walk away, I YELLED, "Hey, Sarge, Sarge I put that cone out there so it would stop anyone, but people in the know from using the lot, and NO ONE had a problem driving around it but you. I'm not here to be the cone guard because some arrogant sergeant needs his ego stroked, SAAAAARGE!" The look on his face was priceless to say the least, and he said NOTHING, just walked away, like the coward that he was. I walked back to Stape who had heard everything, and in his heavy southern accent, he just said, "Damn, boy." I replied with, "Yo, bro, I am FUCKED!" I was just WAITING for unit 1004, my Lieutenant (Lt.), to raise me on the radio for a 5-9 (meet with him) but, the call never came. I was shocked that he didn't immediately go to the Lt. and whine about me calling him out. What that DID tell me was that HE knew that if he had approached the Lt. about what had just occurred, he was going to be ridiculed for his handling of that situation, during what was undoubtedly one of the most stressful times in all of our lives.

Incidentally, the adage about birds of a feather flocking together, he and the aforementioned horrendous sergeant that I worked under after arriving in motors, were best buddies. SHOCKING, I know! Our time at the airport ended fairly quickly, and we tried to get back to some type of normality. I told the previous story not because I was trying to impress you as me being some sort of tough guy that was disrespecting supervisors, because that is not the way that I handled myself. I did respect bosses, even if I thought they had zero redeeming qualities and were horrendous leaders. That story was to illustrate the fact that some of the most severe stress that we encounter in these professions comes not from the streets, but internally, from bosses that don't respect or value their subordinates. In this case, this Sergeant chose to make a stand about me not moving a traffic cone, when he easily could have driven around it, during one of the most tragic times of our lives.

Things had calmed down a little, and we decided to begin playing hockey in early November 2001, which was a welcomed distraction to then current world events, including the US going to war. I had created the team for two reasons; to foster camaraderie amongst the guys on the team and to raise money that could be donated to charitable organizations.

After receiving a huge donation from our biggest sponsor, Solarcom, by its founder and CEO, Eric Prockow, we were up and running. Eric has since passed but was an incredibly warm and generous man! He loved first responders and was always there to help in any way that he could. I was able to get 501(3)C status for the team, which classified it a non-profit and we were on our way to doing fantastic things which included raising $159,000 in three years that were donated to other worthy charities of the team members' choosing. On April 5, 2002, we hosted the FDNY Hockey team at Philips Arena at the conclusion of an Atlanta Thrashers hockey game which was incredible. An estimated 8,000-10,000 people stayed to watch our game, and we were able to raise $25,000, which we donated to the FDNY Widows/Children's Fund. It was an absolutely incredible weekend for everyone involved.

I had called the Atlanta Braves front office and told them about our plan with the FDNY and requested tickets to that weekend's season opening-series between the Atlanta Braves and NY Mets for both of our teams. The Braves promptly said, "Sorry, we cannot help you." On a whim, I then contacted the NY Mets; literally, I just cold-called them to explain what we were doing in Atlanta and requested their help in securing tickets for Saturday nights' Braves-Mets game. Within TEN minutes, I received a call from Jay HORWITZ, the Mets head of public relations, who told me that he had secured FIFTY tickets in the Lexus level for us. I was SHOCKED! I've been remiss in ever sending Jay a thank you card. I still think about it periodically to this day, so Jay, I would like to publicly thank you for what you did for us. It says A LOT about you as a man!

The FDNY manager of the team at the time, Billy Kammerer, said it was the best weekend they'd ever had as a group and thanked us profusely. I would leave the department less than two years later but having to leave that hockey team behind gave me the biggest pause in leaving the Atlanta job and relocating back to New York.

# CHAPTER 10

I had taken the civil service test for the County of Suffolk, NY Police Department sometime in 1996 and scored a 100. I had then been summoned to an informational somewhere in Suffolk County to give all of us who had scored 100 an overview of the impending hiring process in late 1997. Sadly though, we all received very disappointing news a few months later after it was revealed that a certain number of prospective officers had cheated on the autobiographical portion of the test, and although 39,000 people took the test, because that small group of minority cadets cheated, the test was thrown out. Unfortunately, tests are now given that used subjective answers as part of its scoring process, as opposed to the tried and true "right and wrong" answer-based test, although THAT is absolutely another discussion for another book though.

I did go through the hiring process with Suffolk County after re-taking the test in 1999 and scoring a 90. I was hired in October 2003, which was the last class who would get hired from the soon-to-be expired list from that 1999 test. Additionally, there were so many people that scored a 90 on the test (I believe 2,500) that we were all put into a band, and they actually held a pseudo raffle drawing in which names were drawn and only half of that band of 2,500 got the chance to become police officers after undergoing the hiring process. At least when I went through the process many years ago, it was a 10-1 ratio, meaning that for every ten people that began the hiring process, only one would be chosen to enter the academy.

I was presented with a difficult choice in the fall of 2003 when I knew that I had passed all of the testing to enter the Suffolk County Academy. I was also on a short list to go to the K9 Squad at Hartsfield Airport for APD. If accepted, I would have become a K9 handler for an EOD (Explosives & Ordnance Detection) dog and would've been required to attend a 13-week training program at Lackland Air Force Base in Bexar County Texas, where all FAA Certified EOD dogs receive their training. I knew in leaving that the hockey team, which I had built form the ground up, would be left behind, and all my teammates and now friends would be sorely missed. I had recently gotten engaged at that point to a woman would eventually become my ex-wife, but her close family was all located in Atlanta so she was not exactly ecstatic about moving back to New York (she was born in NY but moved to Georgia at the age of five). And truth be told, I was going back to New York MOSTLY for a family that did not value my presence all that much.

The real estate market had skyrocketed in the previous two years so the house that I believed I was going to buy for X amount, was now going to be $200K more than it would have been in 2001. Knowing all of this, I decided that the Suffolk County job would offer me a better quality of life, and I was still trying to be the good son by moving back to be closer to my family.

I began my career with the County of Suffolk Police Department on October 20, 2003, at the Suffolk Co. Police Academy. I had begun running for the academy a couple of months prior to the start, but began experiencing extremely painful shin splints almost immediately, which had sprung up originally during my training at the Atlanta Police Academy more than ten years prior. I realized that if I was to start running a few miles per week that the shin splints were going to be unbearable in a short amount of time, so I made the decision to use the elliptical at my gym to increase my cardio. Looking back, if I had to do it over, I would've begun jumping rope because my cardio was nowhere near what it was during the Atlanta academy, and frankly, nowhere where it should have been as I began Suffolk's.

While it felt good to be back in New York, I was missing Atlanta. I lived with my parents in my childhood during the academy, while my now fiancée stayed back in Atlanta, living in the house we had purchased together about six months earlier. I just kept getting the feeling that I no longer belonged in New York though, and I remember thinking just a short time after moving back to New York that I couldn't wait until retirement so I could get the heck out of there again, forever. Looking back now, isn't that an insane thought to have? I was essentially wishing the next, at a minimum 20 years, away, how is that for living in the present? I realize now that I was not happy back then, and in my soul, I believe that I did not do the right thing in moving back to New York. I did it mainly for two reasons; the first being money, because Suffolk County was one of the highest paid law enforcement jobs in the U.S., and secondly, to be closer to my family which, I realized shortly after being back, was the absolute wrong thing to do.

For any of you who are reading this book and are facing a life altering decision, and the answer to that ever-elusive question of "what is the right answer?" The right answer is the one that will make YOU happy, not your family members, your romantic partner, your friends, etc. The ONLY person that any of us can make happy is ourselves, and if you're making decisions based on what you think others want, or what they think is best for you, disregard it all. You must live with the decisions that you make, not them, and if you're not happy living your day to day, you can be certain that no one else is going to change that. We spend much too much time expending energy worrying about what others may think and have concern about what the effect of our decisions will have on them when I can almost guarantee you, that those same people give little to no credence to what their decisions mean for you.

Additionally, using money as a criterion will almost guarantee that you make the wrong decision in my experience and opinion. Decide what it is that you love, pursue that avenue, and as I've seen repeatedly in my life, the money will follow.

# CHAPTER 11

The Suffolk Academy went by fairly smoothly, we graduated in April 2004, and I was assigned to the 2nd Precinct in Huntington, NY, where I would spend my entire career. I remember as I went through field training, being told how rough a certain area (Huntington Station), of our precinct was and as I was driven through it by one of my field training officers, and thinking to myself, "This is it?" As field training progressed, I was struck by the realization that no one was spitting on the ground as we drove past them. I was not hearing "Fuck the police" multiple times every day, and the craziest thing of all, multiple people actually waved and said, "Thank you, officer," as we went through our day.

It was MUCH different than the streets of Atlanta, and to be honest, it was a much less stressful environment. A man named Jeff Cooper created a "color code," which explains the four levels of "situational awareness" that a police officer prepares for, reference using deadly force. Code white describes a condition in which you are relaxed and unaware of what is going on around you. Police officers should only be in this state when sleeping, but unfortunately, I've seen WAY too many officers who find themselves in this space while wearing the uniform. Condition Yellow is when you are relaxed, but you are aware of who and what is around you. I was certainly NEVER in code white while working in Suffolk, but there was a palpable difference in my stress levels between Atlanta, where I almost found myself at the third threat level—condition

Orange, where you've identified something of interest that may or may not prove to be a threat—and Suffolk County. I never realized how stressful the daily environment was in Atlanta, until I put myself in a different one in Suffolk. It was just my normal, until I found a new normal and realized how abnormal and unhealthy the environment in Atlanta truly was.

Shortly after field training was completed, I was assigned to Squad 3 at the second Precinct on two-tour. On patrol in Suffolk County, our work schedules were broken up into midnight tours, 9:00 p.m.-7:00 a.m., 4 nights on/4 nights off, or two-tour which was 7:00 a.m.-3:00 p.m., 5 days on/2 days off, then 3:00 pm-11:00 pm 5 days on/3 days off. I always hated waking up early, in this case 5:15 a.m. since I always showered and ate breakfast before going to work, but it was usually a slower workday. I preferred the later tours, but that meant that you were going to be working nights on many weekends during the year, and the call volume was usually much higher. Additionally, you will be working many weekends and holidays those first few years until you get some seniority under your belt, and in the case of Suffolk County, since most officers did not retire until they completed their entire 32 (for maximum pension benefits), it could take quite a while. This can be an absolute point of stress for many relationships, since typically, most spouses were working a traditional 9-5 with weekends and holidays off. I've seen spouses who've applied a ton of pressure on their partners to get off for certain events when at times, it's almost impossible to do so. I've also seen officers who let money be their guiding light and work as much overtime as they possibly can without pause to see how negatively it affects their family life. I worked with one guy that I know of, although I GUARANTEE that others have done the same, who came in on CHRISTMAS day because they made double-time-and-a-half since it was their off day and a holiday. Now, if that is something that you absolutely MUST do, then you must handle your business, but I hope they realize that their children are never going to forget that daddy left the family on Christmas day to go to work.

I remember that Suffolk was so slow and uneventful workwise that I had called back to one of my old bosses, a major, and asked him if I I'd be able to slide into that K9 position if I came back to the Atlanta PD. He told me they had just changed the SOP's (Standard Operating Procedures), and you now had to have 3½ years of continuous service on the street before you could go to a specialized detail. Since I had left, I'd have to put in another 3 ½ years before being eligible for K9, ending that possibility rather quickly. Knowing that I was definitely not leaving for at least 20 years, I settled in and began working arduously, learning the culture of another department, becoming proficient in New York law and the various new procedures that I would now be employing in another state.

For the most part, there are many similarities to being an officer in different states, but there are certain nuances in both the cultures, and the laws that can make it drastically different. I had gotten married in June 2004, and we settled in after renting a house in East Meadow, about 30 minutes from work. Unfortunately, adding incredible stress to my life and marriage was the fact that my new wife and mother did not get along well. Unbeknownst to me was that a certain person was so jealous that my mother was possibly going to befriend my new wife, that she set out to sabotage that relationship and made life miserable for everyone in the process.

I will state once again that, regardless of what title they hold, there is no one in your life who is entitled to treat you with any less respect than with which you treat them. I sided with my wife during this early conflict, but I should have taken it further and told my family that if they did not treat her well, they were going to force me to choose between her and them. Looking back now, the behavior exhibited by my mother was extremely selfish, and although she was being encouraged by that other person, she was acting cold and uncaring. Unfortunately, at that time, I was unable to allow myself to be vulnerable and explain to my mother how I felt about the situation. I usually communicated with anger, and the message is rarely received when it is delivered with anger.

Work was going well at this point, but I can clearly remember multiple incidents of responding to aided cases (medical calls), as a now EMT, since we all were EMT-B (Basic EMT) certified officers where people were DOA (Dead on Arrival) and having to tell their loved ones that they were deceased. Many times, people KNOW their loved ones are dead, but they hold out hope, and it does not become reality until we pronounce them dead. I remember one specific incident of a sick elderly woman dying in her bed and her husband pleading with me to tell him that she was "going to make it," only to have to inform him that she had indeed passed away. He was broken-hearted, and it also broke my heart watching him kiss her as she lay in her bed. His daughter came to the house shortly thereafter and told me they were married for an incredibly long amount of time, and she predicted he would not live much longer after that, which he did not. When you leave calls like that, you're not even sure how to process what you just saw. There's no violence involved, and most people would not deem them to be traumatic, but you leave feeling such emptiness and sadness for the husband, in this case.

After that call like so many others, I told NO ONE, not my co-workers, spouse, friends, no one. That is the absolute worst choice that you can make in these emotional experiences. Simply by telling someone what you felt and by lifting that weight off of you, it has been proven in case studies, to be extremely effective and in most cases, people have said that they felt their problem was effectively solved at that point. I would like to say the during the course of my relationship with my ex-wife (19 years), and my subsequent relationship with my current wife, (4 years before re-tirement), I effectively brought home and discussed events that happened to me at work, in length, a handful of times, if that much. I thought that I was protecting my spouse by not talking about the traumatic events at work, but in reality, I was shutting out the person that I was closest to, at that time. We, as first responders speak about the importance of "not bringing that shit home with us," but we're effectively shutting out our significant others about 1/3 of our lives. Traditionally, we as a group are not what you would exactly call the best communicators in the world regarding anything that requires us to be vulnerable, but there is no one that can tell me that the communication with our loved ones is somehow enhanced by us refusing to speak about a large portion of our lives with them. In response to this dilemma, a few months ago, I began to think of a possible solution that I could offer to active-duty personnel to overcome this potential problem. My solution is to sit down with your partner and tell them that you don't want to bring these traumatic things that you experience at work home for the fear of burdening or worrying them, but you also do not want to shut them out so you created a process that you think will work well. Upon returning home from work on a daily basis, you need a little time to decompress before you get into the role of dad or a husband, so the first thirty minutes (or whatever length of time you both agree upon) is yours to decompress and leave work behind, then after that, you are all theirs. If you've had a very traumatic day, however, all that you must do upon walking in the house is say, "Baby, it was a bad one." That's it, nothing else.

From that point forward, the day/night is yours. You can hang out in the man cave, backyard smoking a stogie, whatever the case might be, BUT before your next tour (and if it was your last tour of the set, you have 24 hours), you MUST tell your partner what occurred. Now you do NOT have to get extremely specific. Paint everything in broad strokes, just give a basic outline, or synopsis regarding what you experienced, but they now have a context in which to put your behavior. Instead of "Mike is just an asshole," it is, "Oh, NOW I understand why he…." when they understand that there is an actual factual basis in which to frame your behavior. This doesn't give you an excuse to be an asshole. Never forget that regardless of why you are lashing out, even having a solid contextual reason FOR the behavior, there's absolutely no excuse for the behavior itself.

# CHAPTER 12

The Suffolk job was going great. I got used to the slower pace and realized, I know this sounds funny to most of you reading this, but I began to appreciate not going balls-to-the-wall every day at work. By no means were we dead at work, some days the calls didn't stop the entire tour, but there weren't as many high-priority calls, and the level of violence that I was exposed to in Suffolk County was nowhere near what it was in Atlanta.

As referenced earlier, it actually took a little while for me to not look at the public with such disdain as I did after a couple of years into my career in Atlanta, due to the graciousness of some of the members of the public, such as being thanked for the job that we did, or people attempting to buy us lunch or dinner.

For those of you who've never worn the uniform, when you walk into any type of retail business, or anywhere for that matter, all eyes are on you. It gets a little strange when people graciously offer to pay for our food, as everyone else begins to watch and listen during the interaction, and every single word that you say gets dissected. To all of you that have ever offered to buy me, or any other first responder food, we truly thank you. If at any point during the conversation you felt that we were being ungrateful because we declined the gesture, trust me, we were not, but we feel so awkward when most everyone else in the place knows what's going on that we say, "No thank you." We do, however, walk away from encounters like that feeling supported, and it truly means the world to us, just as a nasty verbal encounter can ruin your day, a gesture like that makes it a beautiful one.

You must get comfortable with people staring at you because you stand out quite a bit when wearing the uniform. To those "comedians" that we encounter, I always wanted to reply to the ever-hilarious line of, "I didn't do it" while raising their hands, "That is fucking hilarious, bro, I've NEVER heard that one before, truly the most creative thing I've heard in a while." While I know that people would find it hard to believe that you must get accustomed to people being nice to you, you are so prepared for the opposite response that it does indeed take a while to acclimate because you had been conditioned to nasty responses for many years.

Unfortunately, I received heartbreaking news in 2005 as I sat in the basement man cave in my house when my ex-wife walked halfway down the stairs, stopped, sat down, and just stared at me with a very hurt look in her eye. I knew that whatever was going to come out of her mouth next was not going to be good, and she said, "Jack Stein just died." Jack was a former teammate and my assistant captain on my Police/Fire ice hockey team, a Gwinnett County, Ga. Police Officer, and we were also great friends with him and his wife.

She went on to explain that Jack had committed suicide early that morning after they had gotten into an argument, he had left the room, ostensibly to sleep in one of the downstairs bedrooms. But when she found Jack the next morning, he had shot himself in the head. Jack had just begun using an anti-depressant that had been prescribed to him during that last week and as is widely known, anti-depressants are known to increase the odds of committing suicide during the early usage period.

I was stunned upon hearing the news, and as my ex-wife cried, I felt such a sadness engulf me, but I was not crying. We flew back to Atlanta a few days later to attend Jack's services, and I was profoundly sad, although I was glad to see a bunch of my old teammates and co-workers who had attended the service.

As I think back on it now, we collectively did not discuss Jack's suicide in depth other than the usual, "I can't believe that he's gone," and "why didn't he reach out to any of us?" If that had happened today, I would have gathered the boys and had a serious talk about mental health. I would've asked anyone if they were struggling, and if they were but didn't want anyone else to know, to pull me aside, or hit me up on the cell.

It is incredible to me how close to the vest that we kept (and most men still do) our emotions, and it's stunning that we will suffer in silence for years, maybe decades, because we will not allow ourselves to be vulnerable enough to ask for help!

I was so sad for a long time after Jack's death, but I could not shed a tear, although I tried MAKING myself and I still could not do it. It actually scared me that I was unable to show emotion regarding this tragedy. I distinctly remember staring at myself in the mirror after a shower during that period, I literally said out loud to myself, "What the fuck is wrong with you? Are you broken?" This, in response to this inability to cry at what was such a personally devastating thing to happen to me. Knowing now what I do about grief and emotions, I realize that I had so thoroughly conditioned myself to staying flat during highly emotional events, whether they be shootings, pursuits, fights, or any other tragic event at work. Situations in which people's lives would be forever irretrievably altered after suffering some type of massive loss, that almost nothing could pierce that veil of armor that I had so thoroughly wrapped around me.

As that event unfolded, I truly believed that I was now broken, and there was no hope for me to be fixed, I had mentally gone past the point of no return. These changes that occur over time are so small and incremental, until one day you find yourself staring in that mirror and you're not even sure who that guy is that's staring back at you. This mental fortitude that allowed me to compartmentalize almost everything in life had served me well, was essential at times, and was hugely beneficial at work in many ways. But it was also incredibly detrimental as well, and in some ways, I was devastated knowing that I was never going to be what I once was. I almost felt like the human version of Humpty Dumpty.

# CHAPTER 13

As I stated earlier, the level of violence that I experienced in Suffolk was drastically less than what I had seen in Atlanta, but we still experienced our fair share. I distinctly remember working a 3-11 tour when one of my co-workers was dispatched to a call of a child who had been accidentally shot in the head while playing with a gun. There were approximately ten units who responded to the call, telling dispatch that they were en route. Five units would've been more than sufficient for that response, and I wanted to yell into the radio to tell the others to disregard, and if it was decided that more officers were needed after our initial response, they could've been requested. I say this because listening to the initial call, coupled with additional updates, it was fairly easy to ascertain that this child was more than likely dead already, and no number of officers sent there was going to be able to affect that outcome.

What many of these officers heading to that call didn't realize was that they were going to be exposed to a very devastating crime scene involving the death of a child and that what they were about to see could not be unseen. There was zero reason to expose themselves to this trauma if they did not have to because a call like this would certainly leave an indelible footprint on them and could potentially cause lasting ill-effects. The child was pronounced dead at the scene, and I remember an officer making a radio transmission advising other units that the parents of the newly deceased child had just gotten to the residence. The victim had been playing at a friend's house and the gun owner's child had gotten the gun out to show the friend. I considered myself lucky to not have been close to the call, thus saving myself horrible memories of seeing those poor parents at that scene, and of having to possibly witness the crime scene itself. I believe that that was the FIRST time in my entire career (probably 13 years at this point) that I was thankful that I did not have to witness a tragedy. It wasn't something that I had ever previously given thought to.

Looking back, I now believe that was also the first time that I had a fleeting thought that all this trauma I had been a part of for the past 13 or so years may have had some sort of negative cumulative effect on my psyche. I cannot, however, tell you that I had looked any further into this concept, or that I made any changes, or attempts to deal with it. It just was what it was.

The next day, I called the officer that had handled that call the previous evening. She was not exactly a battle-hardened individual, and I wanted to speak with her and see how she was feeling after handling such a traumatic event. She had explained to me, in detail, what had taken place and that it had been a devastating scene, I could hear "it" in her voice. She was quite melancholy but said that she was doing fine, and when I told her to speak about it with someone that she felt comfortable talking to, she replied with the perfunctory, "I will." If I had been a little more elevated in my thinking back then, I would've touched base up with her in the days and weeks following, but at the time, I felt like I was intruding.

Looking back on these different events years after they happened, and after cataclysmic changes in my thoughts and beliefs, I now find it incredible that we just compartmentalized (buried) everything that we saw and did and just went on to the next. Rarely, if ever, did we pause for even a minute to process any of what we'd seen or done. The mindset that I, and most everyone I worked with, was it comes with the territory try, not to think about it.

An announcement had come out in the fall of 2007 (I believe), asking for applicants for a newly formed anti-crime team, which really sounded interesting to me as it was going to be a street-level crime suppression unit and the west end team of which I'd be a part encompassed three officers from each of the 1st-4th precincts. The goal was to use us in both a uniformed and undercover capacity to combat various problems, such as drug dealing, street racing, and any other problem that we could address as determined from the powers above.

I immediately applied and was chosen, along with two other guys from my precinct that I got along very well with. Other than one officer from another precinct who said he believed he was applying to a traffic enforcement detail (and who was replaced shortly after we started), everyone there was a hard charger, and it was great to work with them as we all had similar mindsets, including the supervisors, all of whom I LOVED working for.

The detail lasted for approximately three months, and we all had a great time. We worked hard and were assigned to the higher crime areas of the four precincts on the west end of the county, though we primarily worked in the first precinct, which had quite a high crime rate. It was a great time as we were all super active, enjoyed working as a group, and you felt like you were at least slightly impactful, performing actual police work.

Unfortunately, the detail lasted only three months, but it rejuvenated me in terms of me enjoying the job. Police work ebbs and flows, for the most part I've always loved it, but you get stale periodically and need a change from the day to day. I know that sounds strange when you're talking about a job in which things can go from boring to deadly in the snap of a finger, but that detail put some pep in my step again.

# THE RESILIENT WARRIOR

# CHAPTER 14

I had suffered from back problems ever since the age of 19, when I got injured doing straight-legged deadlifts at the gym. The chiropractor told me that I had tight hamstrings which limited my pelvic mobility, and this caused my lower back to over-compensate which led to various injuries. I had been battling them on and off for years and would be prescribed medication for the pain, which at times, became unbearable.

Ever since 2000, I would be prescribed Tramadol. It did not bother my stomach like Vicodin, did not seem as harsh a painkiller as it was legal to purchase online, and its effects would last much longer than most any other painkiller than I'd ever been prescribed. I honestly enjoyed the euphoric feeling that it gave me, but I'd always taken it as prescribed and had never abused it. Furthermore, my drug usage consisted of smoking marijuana a handful of times in high school, and I'd always been fervently anti-drugs. To this day, I've never even seen cocaine in my private life. I've encountered it plenty of times at work but have never seen it at a party, or otherwise.

I say that because I would estimate that sometime in 2009-ish, my marriage was not going well. I'm not going to delve too deeply into it, but one of the problems was the lack of graciousness that my mother, and certainly my ex-sister showed towards my then wife. She had left her close family in Atlanta to follow me to New York, and I had hoped for them to become close, but everything was about my mom unfortunately, and she was quite selfish towards my wife. Instead of extending my ex-wife some empathy and grace, there was always some issue about her somehow offending my mother. I tried to mediate, but my mother was less concerned about making my wife feel welcomed by her than any of the other issues that she had a problem with. Adding fuel to the fire was her daughter's jealousy at possibility of my ex-wife and mother possibly having a close relationship, which she sabotaged every time she could. I attempted to broker peace and make both my ex and my mother happy, but no one was, least of all me.

I had no answers, and I could see this issue, amongst others, starting to affect my marriage. What I also noticed, however, was that the Tramadol dulled the pain of everything going on around me. Instead of trudging through my day, I was falsely feeling euphoric due to this medicine. I remember running out of it one time, and I said to myself, "Do you want to renew your scrip and be happy for three weeks, or do you want to deal with these issues?" Well, the answer was simple for me; I just refilled the scrip. I had my primary care doctor prescribing it regularly, and if I needed more, I was able to purchase it legally online, and I didn't have to deal with the pain and drama that was occurring around me. No one had noticed any significant changes regarding my personality, and while I cannot say that I was happy at this point, I thought I was happier than if I wasn't taking the pills. Don't get me wrong, at some point, I realized that I needed them since I had developed a physical dependency, but I bargained with myself saying that they weren't that bad since I could legally purchase them online. I had only run out of them one time when FedEx had missed a delivery and that night I was tossing, turning in my bed, and DT'ing (detoxing) when I realized that I was addicted to Tramadol.

That feeling is inexplicable to someone who's never felt it. You literally feel like you're crawling out of your skin, and you are flipping over in bed about every five seconds since you cannot stop moving, which is not an exaggeration. To this day, I don't know how my wife slept as I tossed and turned all night. I would take enough pills with me to work so that I didn't feel any sickness, and no one would ever notice that I was taking them. Truth be told, some days I took up to FIFTY pills, and no one had ever noticed anything, even the fact that I had been losing weight to the point that I had gotten down to 205 lbs., which I hadn't been in over 20 years.

The scary part is that Tramadol has the potential to cause seizures in adults who consume more than eight pills/day, and over the course of three years, I had suffered a total of eight seizures from the incredible amounts that I was ingesting. On one particular January day, while my then-wife was in Europe on business, I remember walking towards my countertop, then the next thing I remember is removing some of my wife's clothes from her closet and placing them on our bed upstairs.

As I became more lucid, I felt massive pain on the left side of my face and upon looking in the bathroom mirror, I saw that the entire left side of my face was discolored, and my left eye was black and blue and partially closed. I quickly realized that I had suffered a seizure in the kitchen, fell, and struck my face on the granite countertop and probably almost died. My Rottweiler, Anna, had been lying just under the counter where I had fallen, and if I had hurt her, I don't know what I would've done. I certainly would've never forgiven myself.

Incredibly though, that did not stop me. As it was mid-January, it was easy to take vacation days and I took the whole set off, five days, and spent the next ten days in the house so no one could see what my face looked like. My wife was away the entire time, so absolutely no one knew about that incident.

Looking back now, it is incredible to me that I didn't reach out and ask for help because I certainly needed it. I believe it was $1\frac{1}{2}$ more years before I had my eighth and final seizure one Sunday night as we watched television in the man cave. My wife had run across the street and gotten our neighbors after I began having a seizure, and I asked them to excuse us at which time I told her that I needed help and that I was addicted to the pills. She was relieved that I finally admitted it and called my cousin Tim, who had come over about midnight and slept over the house to keep an eye on me, which I'll never forget.

The next morning, I called her uncle who was in the healthcare field and had a good friend (I'll call her Sue) that owned an out-patient rehabilitation facility. We went there for a meeting with Sue later that morning and she recommended an in-patient program to detox me, due to the insane amount of Tramadol that I had been consuming. Sue was going to handle the insurance, and hopefully, I'd be approved to enter an inpatient program the following day.

It was then time to break the news to my parents as they had absolutely no idea what had been going on. All three of us rang the bell and my mother was quite confused as to the purpose of all three of us being there and I explained everything. If there was another time in my life where I was more humiliated and embarrassed, I certainly cannot recall it. My father reacted with typical anger, the exact opposite emotion of how I'd hoped he'd react, but I was certainly not surprised that he didn't offer a hug and promise of "it will be okay," which is exactly what I had needed at that time.

We received a call later that day from Sue who said that she had just concluded a conference call with several high-level Blue Cross executives as they had initially denied my treatment since I was the first member that they'd ever had who'd suffered an addiction to Tramadol. I was shocked at that statement since Tramadol is synthetic Codeine, had been classified a controlled substance shortly after this, and I do not believe it would've received this classification had it not been abused by others. Again, I'm in no way excusing my behavior by stating others had been addicted, only that I find it hard to believe that I was the only member of Blue Cross to have an addiction to this medicine.

After a long night, I reported to the facility in the Hamptons the following day and I remember that first night as I sat in bed in a room that I shared with three other guys, I cried and asked myself, "How the fuck did you get here?" I vowed that I would never allow myself to get addicted to anything ever again, and that I was going to lead a productive life from here on in. I stayed in the facility for 2½ weeks, then left on Labor Day Monday. I began my outpatient program the following week and graduated from the program three months later.

The one great thing that happened was that I had blown out my back at work in late June and had been out long-term, line-of-duty injury the entire time I had been in rehab. As a result, no one at work ever found out except one very close buddy, so I never had to battle the stigma of having been to rehab. Let mine be a cautionary tale to anyone because as I said, I was a fervent anti-drug guy, and if it could happen to me, it could happen to anyone. I had zero idea that years later this experience would give me the ability to speak to others who've gone down this road, and for them to be able to easily identify with me to help them.

An incredible side note was that I had received a call from my ex-wife in early December while at work and she was furious, as well as hurt. She proceeded to tell me that she had just received a phone call from my mother, out of the blue wherein my mother berated her for MY painkiller addiction and told her that it was her fault that it had occurred. I was blown away at the gall of my mother, and the fact that she had blamed anyone else but me and was disgusted and furious that she had the audacity to make accusations like that towards my ex-wife. It was an extremely selfish act. My ex-wife stated that she did not want to spend Christmas with my family and it was up to me if I would so. I immediately called my mother and expressed my extreme unhappiness at the disgusting thing she'd just done while informing her that I would be spending Christmas with my ex-wife's family after what she had done.

I remember how happy I was to get my life back, which is truly how I felt at that point. All you want to do is scream from the rooftops that you are clean and that you got your life back, but at the same time, you keep it all under wraps except for those closest to you. I remember telling one or two of my closest friends what had been happening, and they were literally in shock, due to my stance against drugs.

My mom and dad had told none of our relatives at that point, and I told my mom to tell my aunt and uncle on each side just in case someone else in the family was going through something similar, and my story could help them in some way. I had mostly gotten over the embarrassment and humiliation, but I still had to forgive myself and that was not going to be as easy. I replayed how far I'd fallen thousands of times in my mind until one day, I realized, "this is doing you no good." I told myself; this is not you; it is something you did, and you did it to avoid pain. But I had to come to terms with it, put it to bed, and finally forgive myself.

One habit that really kicked into high gear while I was taking the pills was self-isolating. I would spend a great portion of my day in the "man cave" and not socializing with friends and that is without a doubt, one of the worst things one can do. In the case of depression, which I was potentially suffering from, you constantly have negative thought patterns and low energy, and it is just more comfortable to isolate yourself. As a result, you don't have to explain why you're quieter than usual, or why you aren't in the mood to do xyz. You're vibrating on that lower energy frequency scale and engaging in conversation, and being entertaining is not at the top of your list at that point. You're just trying to make it through your day. However, humans are social animals that cannot live in isolation or loneliness. As the Greek philosopher Aristotle said,

"Man is by nature a social animal; an individual who is unsocial naturally and not by accident is either beneath our notice or more than human." This essentially means that man is a social animal and anyone who is not naturally is either a beast or a God because they do not participate in the shared life of a community.

When I went back to work about two weeks later, I kept waiting for someone to tap me on the shoulder at work to discuss it, but no one ever did. I recommitted myself to being a great officer at work because I had been slacking for quite some time. I was never derelict in handling my duties. As I said, no one had noticed anything, but in my mind, I knew that I was not holding myself up to the standards that I was used to.

Approximately three months later, I had an extremely powerful conversation with one of my friends, Craig Capolino, which forever shaped my view on a few things. Craig was a former narcotics detective with the NYPD, and he and I attended the Suffolk police academy together. Although we were eventually assigned to different precincts, we reunited on that anti-crime squad in 2007 that I had spoken about earlier. Craig had been diagnosed with 911-related cancer, and his diagnosis was terminal. We used to speak very frankly about life and death, and Craig ALWAYS had a positive attitude and a smile on his face. I truly loved that kid!

During this particular conversation, Craig had revealed some unfortunate news regarding his illness and how he'd love more time on this earth. As soon as he said that, I thought about my stint in rehab approximately three months earlier and I just began to cry. I was so embarrassed about doing so, and I immediately muted the phone so that he would not hear me. Whenever he had finished his last thought, there was silence on the phone as I was still unable to compose myself. Craig finally called my name, believing that we had been disconnected and to this day, I don't know why I didn't hang up, pretend that I was in a bad reception area, and call him back after I had stopped crying, but I didn't. I hit the mute button again and started speaking as well as I could, which was not that great. Craig could tell I was crying, and he immediately became alarmed, asking me, "Mike, what's the matter?" I replied that I was a piece of shit. I told him the story of my painkiller addiction in its entirety, then told him, "You're fighting for one more day on this earth every day, and I was throwing my life away isolating myself downstairs in my basement taking painkillers!"

Craig was super compassionate, and asked me if I was clean, and I replied, "100% brother." He said, "That's all that matters Mike, you made a mistake, and I know it's not you; you have a lot to give to this world." I actually started crying harder at that point, but finally, I was able to compose myself, and I told him, "I know I fucked up, brother, but I promise you that I'm going to lead a productive life from here on out. I want you to look down and be proud of me, and I will never waste my life again."

Craig went on to tell me that he knew that I would and to forgive myself. I had mentioned to Craig that it was incredible to me that he never said that he had never felt sorry for himself. He never echoed a victim vibe in any conversation that we had, ever. He asked me "why shouldn't I get cancer, people get diagnosed with cancer every day, and what's so special about me that I should not contract it." That attitude BLEW me away and his awareness and emotional IQ were both off the charts. We all could learn something from Craig's perspective on life. Craig Capolino passed away in January 2013, and he will forever be missed by many, especially me.

# CHAPTER 15

One of the main things that is preached during the course of a rehabilitation program is to not make any life-altering decisions for approximately twelve months after you conclude your rehab program. Although this book is certainly not a guide to having a successful marriage, after becoming sober, I think in the back of my head I knew that my marriage was not going to last. I NOW know after much introspection over the past few years that I entered it without ever being in love with my ex-spouse. I "loved" her, but don't believe I was ever "IN love" with her, and I truly believe that you need that foundation to fall back on when you go through difficult times.

I finally concluded only about a year or so ago that I stayed with her because I loved her family. Her mother and stepdad gave me so much love from day one and always treated me with the utmost kindness, generosity, love and respect, and I absolutely loved both of them. It was something that I had never felt from my own family, and although her stepfather was one of the most intelligent men I've ever had the pleasure of knowing in my life, he would sit and talk and listen to me, my thoughts, my opinions, and that is something that my father never did in my life.

I certainly would never preach to anyone, but if you ever have a doubt deep in your soul that someone is not right for you, sit with it and truly find out why it doesn't feel right. Talk to your friends, be honest with them, as well as yourself. Sometimes people are great individuals but that doesn't necessarily mean they're going to be a great couple. We never had a contentious relationship. We just became roommates, and life is too short to go through it unhappily.

I still wanted to do my best to try and make our marriage work, but I certainly was not what one would call emotionally intelligent at that point in my life. Do not confuse Intelligence Quotient (IQ) with Emotional Quotient (EQ); they are two distinct concepts. IQ is our ability to think logically, comprehend and assimilate new information, and problem-solve. EQ refers to our ability to recognize and manage our own emotions and the emotions of others.

Growing up I was never taught to express my emotions without being ridiculed or belittled. Consequently, I suppressed my feelings and felt weak if I was expressing anything other than happiness or anger. I was always a funny guy, so my sense of humor deflected most of my hurt, and anger was always there to be called upon when I needed it, because I certainly was never going to acknowledge the fact that someone had hurt me. That lack of emotional intelligence though is so devastating to one's growth and progress in life, and it never allows you to truly reach your potential in so many ways.

I got back into exercising hard at the gym and realized that both my mental and physical health went hand in hand. The gym, which I always had a love/hate relationship with, became my 90 minutes of daily meditation and I began to love training. To this day, I need to work out to keep my mind clear and focused, and that discipline spreads to so many other parts of your life.

Work was going well, although the traumatic events never stopped, nor will they ever in that profession. One story just came to mind that made me stop after the call was completed to acknowledge the pain that I had felt for the couple involved. I had received a report of a motor vehicle accident with injuries at Commack Rd.

and the North Service Rd. of the LIE (Long Island Expressway), an intersection that was notorious for car accidents.

Upon my arrival, I observed a damaged vehicle that was stopped, facing the wrong way on an inclined portion of grass at the intersection. There were multiple civilians on scene already, and as I approached, I could see that the driver's door was heavily damaged, necessitating the "Jaws of Life" to open the door. As I got closer though, I could see that the elderly driver was dead, his eyes were wide open, and he was staring blankly ahead. Tragically, his wife was sitting in the front passenger seat next to her dead husband. She was fully awake and conscious and appeared to seemingly be uninjured, but her car door was also damaged and unable to be opened.

For the next 20 minutes as the Fire Department and our police Emergency Service Units attempted to extricate this poor woman from the vehicle, she had to sit next to her deceased husband. She was quite stoic through the entire ordeal, but I just could not imagine being in her position. I had no idea how long the couple had been together, but odds are that it was a very long time, and this was the way it was going to end, truly heartbreaking. The detectives came out to the scene to investigate the accident and as I updated them, none of us were in the mood for the morbid jokes that we usually tell to break the massive tension that engulfs scenes like this. It was just another reminder for all of us that life is a precious gift, and none of us is immune to tragedy.

We did not experience loss solely outside of our department; there was plenty to go around internally as well. During the course of about five to eight years in my precinct alone, in addition to tragically losing a great guy, Officer Glen Ciano, who died while on-duty when his patrol car was struck by a DWI driver, hit a pole, and burst into flames, we had lost four additional officers, three by suicide, and another who was killed in an off-duty car accident.

The suicides were spoken about shortly after they occurred, but as time passed, they faded away, almost as if the officers never existed. All three were traced back to failing domestic relationships, but I could never reconcile the fact that people chose such a permanent solution to a temporary problem. I always wondered if people who committed suicide thought about the lasting impacts on their families. We often hear that their rationale was that they were a burden to their family and that their families would be better off without them. The reality is though, most of those children will grow up wondering if they were the cause of their parent's suicide, or if they were loved by their parent because who would do that to a child that they loved, they're transferring that burden onto their child for the remainder of their lives. The trauma experienced by these children is immeasurable and things like this lead to generational trauma, substance abuse, and domestic abuse in the case of kids who grow up feeling unworthy of love, then choosing less-than-healthy partners as a result. There are so many incredibly detrimental long-term effects experienced by family members of people who commit suicide, not to mention, friends and associates.

One of my main missions in writing this book is to try and reach that one person who is reading this while experiencing suicidal ideation in his/her life in the hope that they will identify with some of the issues I discuss, and they realize they're not alone, far from it actually. Although I've never had any suicidal ideations, I've experienced depression and been in that vicious cycle where one negative thought springboards you into the deep end of ruination. To any of you who are experiencing these thoughts, remember this, the same mind that put you into that negative cycle of thought is the exact same mind that can get you out of it. Your perception of life dictates your mindset and your actions, and if you learn to live a life of gratitude wherein you are thankful for everything that you have, as opposed to thinking about all of the things that you don't, you will live a happy life. Learn to replace those negative thoughts that enter your head immediately with positive ones, and soon the negative thoughts will appear less often and will be quick to be eradicated when they do appear. I believe there's both an arrogance and fear associated with suicide. Some people believe that they're too strong for something like that to happen to them, and others are fearful and think that "if it could happen to them, it could happen to me." I can't imagine that people who get to that point are in their "right minds," otherwise they would never complete the act, but I can't imagine how profound the pain they're experiencing to believe that suicide is a better answer than any other available solution. I do know that I never want to experience the suicide of a friend, family member, or associate ever again. I've already seen a lifetime full of them.

# CHAPTER 16

I will now recount the story of what I consider to be my craziest call in my entire 30-year career. It took place on a cold Sunday night as I worked a 3-11 pm tour. It had been a relatively slow night up until that point (as every cop knows, you NEVER mention that your day/night is "dead," or else all hell will break loose), and we were about to "clear a meal" (have dinner) approximately 15 minutes from then, at 8:00 (2000 hours military time) when the radio came to life. Dispatch had raised unit 219 to start for a 10, which is a motor vehicle accident, but 219 had cleared a meal herself a short time before that, so typically, if it's just a minor call, the adjoining sector unit would handle it. This allows unit 219 to stay on her meal, and in theory, if I was on my meal later that night and had received a minor call, unit 219, or whomever, would pick that call up for me, thus allowing me to finish my meal.

I told dispatch to keep 219 on her meal, and I would handle the MVA. My buddy, who just happened to be with me, told dispatch that he would back me up on the call and we began to drive over to the scene, which was very close to our current location. As I drove north on Deer Park Ave., I could see what appeared to be a simple "rear-ender" on the southbound side involving two vehicles and made a U-turn shortly thereafter. As I pulled up, I parked right behind the involved vehicles in the middle lane, a right-turn-only lane began just after my vehicle. My partner Frankie had to use the bathroom, so he had stopped at the firehouse since we were in that parking lot when the call was first dispatched. I walked up the driver's side of the vehicles and saw the driver still seated in the first vehicle, who had rear-ended the vehicle in front of his. The driver had apparent blood on his T-shirt and a deployed air bag, so I assumed (INCORRECTLY) that was what had caused the blood to be on his shirt. The second driver, an Asian male had exited his car and had intercepted me before I could speak to the driver of the first vehicle. The Asian male did not speak good English but kept repeating the phrase, "He hit me," and after about the fifth time he had said it, I told him, "Yeah bro, I understand."

I turned back to the driver still seated in the vehicle and asked him if he was okay. He responded in a very slurred speech, and I asked, "You're drunk, bro?" He just stared at me. I asked him how many drinks he had consumed, and he replied he didn't know. As I said earlier, if someone is on a meal and a minor call gets dispatched in their sector, other units usually pick it up as I did, but this had now become a DWI investigation, and probable arrest so I advised dispatch to "have 219 come to the scene." Unfortunately for her, 219 was going to have to handle the DWI arrest, but I would still handle the accident itself.

My partner, Frankie, then arrived on scene simultaneously with one of the fire chiefs as an additional caller had called 911 and reported it as an accident with injuries triggering a fire department response. Frankie blocked the right-turn lane with his car, and after I had updated him, he walked over to update the fire chief. I began to walk up the passenger side of the involved vehicles, and as I did, I observed the still-seated driver reach over to the passenger side seat, and as his arm came back towards his seat, I could clearly see a knife in his right hand. Next, incredibly, I saw him plunge the knife into his neck, and as I ran up to the passenger side front door, I yelled over to Frankie who was still speaking to the fire chief, "Frankie, he's trying to kill himself."

I attempted to open the door, but he immediately locked it, at which time I ran around the front of the car to his door, but before

I could open it, he locked it. I immediately pulled out my flashlight, very happy with my decision to always replace my flashlight end caps with window punches, and I struck his window with it, which immediately caused it to fold over inside his vehicle. Unfortunately, when it did that it covered the door handle so I could not reach in and open the door, additionally, his door locks were completely flush when locked so I was unable to pull it up to unlock the door. I immediately thought of the blood on his shirt and realized that the air bag had not caused that injury; he had cut his neck after getting in the MVA.

What I did not know at the time was that the officer in the sector adjoining mine had arrested this man for DWI the night before, he had resisted, and they had gotten into a physical confrontation. His vehicle had been parked in a parking lot at another fire station nearby the night before, and after he bonded out of jail earlier that day, he had started drinking heavily.

He then did something I will never forget until the day I die. He put the knife inside of his neck wound after he had cut his neck and began simultaneously sawing the knife as he pulled his skin away from his body. It was incredible. I was thinking very calmly throughout the entire incident and knew that if I didn't intercede that he would kill himself, so I thought about breaking the glass of his rear door and entering the car. If he somehow had gotten the "jump on me" and stabbed me, forcing me to use deadly force, would I be questioned as to why I entered the car, so I decided to deploy my taser. The problem was that it was a winter night, and he was wearing a baggy jacket. When you deploy a taser, both prongs must seat themselves in a person's skin and that jacket would've precluded that from happening. I decided I had to shoot high, and striking someone above the neck is extremely frowned upon, but I believed this to be the less of two evils since he was surely going to kill himself if given enough time.

I deployed the taser and one prong struck him in the left side of his neck, and the other, the left side of his forehead. When it happened, the scene from *The Hangover* popped in my head where Zack Galifikanakis got shot in the head by the kid at the police station, and Rob Riggle yelled "In the face!" When you taser someone, each trigger pull causes a shock cycle lasting five seconds, but the muscles contract heavily, and he only held the knife harder so after those five seconds, he would begin stabbing himself (now he was stabbing the knife up and down the right side of his face) again.

The fire chief with Frankie had broken the passenger-side window with his ax wherein Frankie deployed his taser and those prongs landed on the right side of his neck and forehead. The problem was that as soon as one cycle had ended, he began furiously stabbing himself again, and I was thinking about what other solution would work.

Finally, I pulled my ASP out and I started hitting him as hard as I could in the left side of his face. FINALLY, the pain threshold became too much, and he just stopped, dropped the knife, and exited the car. He said NOTHING the entire time this was taking place; no yelling, no screaming, absolutely nothing, even when he exited the car and I handcuffed him quickly, he said nothing.

The on-scene paramedic looked at his wounds and declared miraculously that nothing vital was struck. He was wrapped up and transported to Good Samaritan Hospital. The funny part was that the charge nurse in the hospital got so angry wanting to know "why did those officers tase this poor man in the head" before she had heard anything about what had happened. Here we just saved this gentleman's life and nurse Rachett is ready to make a complaint without having any information whatsoever in which to put the context of why he was tasered in the head/neck twice.

I cannot say that the call was overly traumatic for either of us. Perhaps if we did not have as much experience as we did, it would have been, but other than us speaking between ourselves about how insane the entire call had been, there was no debrief, no one asked how we were doing, and had we not had been taking a meal right afterwards, we would've gone right back into service. Although that call was certainly not the norm, and even compared to other chaotic calls, that one stands alone. It was still part and parcel for the job.

# CHAPTER 17

The next call that I'm going to talk about affected me like no other. It was literally the one call in my 30-year career in which I cried. I had buried this call for years afterwards, until it surfaced five years later in a way that I had not seen coming, and essentially, blew open Pandora's Box for me.

It was July 2018, and I was working a 3-11 tour in my normal 220 car. It was a beautiful sunny early evening when the dispatcher raised me for an aided case in my sector, and then followed it up with, "A two-year-old found floating in a pool." I was in my patrol car and immediately began heading to the call. I was approximately a mile-and-a-half away and proceeded northbound on Deer Park Ave, then turned eastbound on the LIE S Service Rd. I was pushing the car as fast as it would go. I was traveling about 120 mph. I had actually passed by my sergeant who was also responding.

I was probably on-scene in (2) minutes, and as I pulled up, I was very happy to see Billy Stio pulling up with me. Billy was a former Fire Chief for the Dix Hills volunteer fire department, as well as an Emergency Services police officer with the Nassau County PD, our neighboring police department. Billy is as solid as they come, and he's one of only a handful of guys that I would've wanted next to me in a super intense call like this. Billy had responded to the call directly from his house, which is how he arrived so quickly, and he had gone into the backyard ten seconds ahead of me.

When I ran into the yard, Billy was performing compressions on the baby's back in an attempt to bring her back to life. She was a beautiful little girl named Dana Sikorsky. As intense as this incident was, I was calmly speaking to Billy, offering to take over if he got tired and telling him that he was doing a great job.

Finally, the baby began breathing again, but we had no idea how long she had been on the water. The ambulance arrived on scene, and we quickly ran to the front with her, handed her off, and the rescue crew brought Dana and her parents into the ambulance and took off. I had asked the ambulance what their route was going to be and then broadcast that over the radio in an attempt to get units to pertinent locations to stop traffic for the transport. This is not our typical procedure, but in dire cases, we will provide this service for the ambulance. One of the sergeants had gotten on the radio and asked the third precinct for help as most of the route was going to be in their jurisdiction and they responded impressively.

Once the ambulance had gone, I began focusing on the task at hand, which included notifying detectives of the incident as they had to come to the scene and investigate any possible negligence involved in the incident, and if Dana had passed, a death investigation. We were absolutely unsure at that point if Dana would survive, but the odds were definitely not in her favor since no one knew how long she had been in the water.

As I spoke to the remaining adults at the party, which included Dana's grandparents, we surmised that the family was having a small get-together, and the kids had been playing in the pool. They then exited the pool and had gone inside the house to play in the basement. As a result, the grandparents, who had been tasked with watching the children, had gone inside the house also, one floor above the children. No one had realized it, but Dana had accessed a rarely used door in the basement and had gone back into the backyard. She had apparently fallen into the pool at some point, where her grandfather had eventually found her, but for how long she had been in the pool, no one knew.

For the next three hours or so, as detectives took statements, and crime scene took photos and collected evidence, I had to listen the most visceral screams and cries from Dana's grandparents, who were more than likely blaming themselves for what had just taken place. I had never had the feeling of me crawling out of my skin before or since this incident in my entire life, but I wanted to be anywhere in the entire world other than that backyard at that time. I remember at one point that listening to their cries was literally breaking my heart, and my eyes had begun welling up with tears.

In my entire 25-year career up to that point, and never again afterwards, had I ever cried on a call. I began walking behind some bushes in the backyard because I didn't want anyone to see me crying when I suddenly stopped and said to myself, "You can't fucking cry you fucking pussy, If I cry, they're gonna be worse and they're gonna think I'm a pussy!" I literally said those words to myself and immediately stopped crying. Letting myself go and allowing myself to feel the pain I was experiencing and allowing that release would've been the best thing I could've done for myself, but "men don't cry." I've been told that since I was a little boy. So instead of having some type of cathartic release, absolutely 100% natural in this situation, I compartmentalized the pain that I was feeling, put it in that proverbial box that we use, and BURIED it!

We had gotten a few updates on Dana's condition throughout the evening, but it was still touch and go at that point, and I cannot say that I was optimistic. I remember returning home from work that night to an empty apartment as my then-wife and I had recently separated at that point, and every time I began to think about Dana, I switched my thoughts to something else entirely. I just would not allow myself to think about it. In Suffolk, at the end of our tours, we changed over our cars at "relief points" throughout the county, most of which being fire houses, the logic being that instead of calling all units into the precinct for roll call, it is more efficient to leave them scattered throughout the precinct to answer calls in a timely manner. When I went on duty the next day at my relief point, I was advised by my dispatcher to make a 12, which meant to go to the precinct. It's funny, because anytime you receive a 12 unexpectedly, the first thing you think to yourself is, "What did I do?" I scanned my memory quickly and could not recall any reason for a 12, certainly not for any recent mistake on my part.

Upon arriving at the precinct, I was told by my sergeant that the department had provided the chaplain for me to speak to about the traumatic call that I had experienced the night before involving Dana. I thank the department for providing the chaplain, but it certainly was not an adequate enough response. A therapist, counselor, or a psychologist experienced in trauma-based issues should have been brought to the precinct, not a priest. That is absolutely no-knock on the chaplain, only that he was ill equipped, in my humble opinion, to adequately assess and provide the proper guidance in that situation.

He asked me how I was doing, and I replied with the usual, "I'm okay, father." I had told him about the call and was detailed in my explanation, telling him everything except for the fact that I had begun crying on the call. I had questioned why God had allowed that baby to be brought back to life if she was only going to be in a vegetative state, which was the prognosis at that point due to Dana having suffered a hypoxic brain injury.

The chaplain said that he understood my logic but to think about it this way, "If it's God's will that Dana is to die, at least you gave the family time to grieve with her." I told him I understood that, but I will not understand if he lets her live only to be in a vegetative state. He told me that he understood my concern, but that it was not my choice to make, at which time I told him that if it did happen that way, I was going to be mad at God. We ended our talk shortly thereafter, and I can honestly say that speaking to the chaplain had done nothing to help my mindset. In fact, it had gotten worse.

I started struggling because I began feeling guilty for saving this poor baby if she was only going to be in a vegetative state, and then I felt even stronger guilt for feeling the original guilt, although I would've have saved her life 1,000 out of 1,000 times if I had to do it again. The dynamics of the emotions I was feeling were incredible, and I didn't feel like I could talk to anybody. I was not strong enough to allow myself to feel vulnerable enough to express my emotions to anyone.

Miraculously, a few days later, it was determined that Dana had pulled through and although her future was unknown, she was a fighter and had survived what most kids would not have. Scott Dipino, the then chief of the fire department, had kept me up to date on Dana's condition as he had developed a rapport with Dana's father. Dana was eventually brought home from the hospital, and she faced a long road of recovery ahead, but her family was so appreciative they had their baby, regardless of her suffering brain damage. It was very beautiful to see.

Scott had told me many times that Dana's father had asked me to stop by but, truth be told, I was so afraid of seeing her, then bursting into tears that I would just placate Scott by telling him that I would do so when I got a chance. Between the guilt I had still felt for saving Dana, compounded by guilt for those feelings, then my worry about keeping my shit together when I saw her, I would not allow myself to go to their house.

Compounding problems, however, was that I had two drug addicts living across the street from the Sikorsky's and every single time a call to that address was dispatched, I became enraged because I knew eventually I was going to run into Dana's family. I remember one particular call that I responded to and when I entered the apartment alone, there were about ten "skels" (slang for drug addicts) inside. When told of the usual nonsense that had brought me there, I lost my shit and told them that I would take all ten of them on right there, and there was very colorful language involved. I may not be the baddest dude in the world, but they weren't exactly UFC level fighters and between me seeing red due to the Sikorskys possibly inviting me inside their home, and this nonsense, I was ready to roll.

Unfortunately, during one of these nonsensical calls at this house it happened. Mr. Sikorsky saw me and invited me into their home. I accepted and when I entered Dana's bedroom, I was met by her mother, older sister, Dana's nurse, and Dana who was lying in a hospital bed unable to track my movements with her eyes. I was updated on her condition, which was better than expected, but there was still a long way to go for a full recovery. I began to feel my eyes welling up with tears and pretended that whatever radio traffic was currently going on was for me then grabbed my microphone, pretending to copy a call even though none was being dispatched before I quickly excused myself and left the house. I told myself that I could not go in there again. It was just a heartbreaking scene for me, and I experienced so many emotions after seeing Dana.

To make matters worse, I had received a notification sometime that fall that myself, Billy, and the rescue squad was going to receive an award for saving Dana's life. I remember thinking to myself, "I don't want an award for this!" More guilt was then heaped on me, and I struggled with declining the award, but there were many more people involved than just me, and it seemed disrespectful to decline it. I remember going to the awards presentation one particular evening, wracked with guilt though I told no one, not even my now-wife who I had just begun dating about two months earlier. The entire night I just kept asking myself, "What the fuck am I doing here?"

Calls like this need to be felt and processed out. Even if I would've just spoken with co-workers, I believe that I would've released that burden that I was feeling and I would've gotten that 1,000-pound weight off my chest. The worst thing you can do is exactly what I had done, bottled it up, and suppressed it so that I could avoid feeling that pain. You avoid nothing, however, as it is now a part of your psyche and you cannot unring that bell once it's rung.

We cannot run from these things that haunt and hurt us. We must heal from them, and when you do, you become a stronger, more resilient person, who's capable of helping others and who's capable of having healthy relationships. I was not yet at that point in my life though, not even close. To be honest with anyone reading this book, as I typed this chapter, I cried several times as it is still an emotional subject for me, even seven years later. Although I now allow myself to feel vulnerable and in addition to even allowing myself to cry, I am certainly no longer embarrassed at having done so and am very proud that I am able to show and feel emotion.

# THE RESILIENT WARRIOR

# CHAPTER 18

Things had been going pretty smoothly until we turned the page to the calendar to the year 2020, when all of our lives would take a dramatic turn that no one saw coming. My work life was upended in a dramatic fashion, causing me to lose my "work husband" and closest confidante literally overnight.

The COVID virus, first seen in early January, had been infecting more and more Americans until March when severe lockdowns started to be put into place. I was not too worried. It appeared to be more of a severe flu than anything catastrophic, but precautions had been put in place, increasing in severity as the number of victims of the illness started ramping up. At work, we were now forced to wear masks. We were told to stop enforcing vehicle and traffic law as traffic stops would only increase our interactions with the public, resulting in more officers becoming infected. Additionally, the two-man cars that we ran were split up and each officer from that unit would drive his own patrol car, even though they were going to the same calls all day, every day. That rule change in particular got to me. Logically speaking, the officers might not have been patrolling in the same car all day, but they were together all day anyway, so the likelihood of one passing it to another was still astronomically high. Life changed instantaneously for all of us when COVID came calling.

Unknown to me at the time was that my "partner" (we rode in separate cars but were together 90% of the time) had suffered some sort of COVID Psychosis causing him to suddenly be missing from work. I attempted to reach him and was receiving no response. When I spoke to my sergeant, who had been aware of what was going on, he was forced to keep it to himself and made up a story of family turmoil. I finally received a call from a very close mutual friend who brought me up to speed, leaving me absolutely speechless as my buddy was now hospitalized. I told my sergeant that he could talk to me now because I was fully aware of the situation. He responded with, "Thank God I can talk to you now. This had been the hardest two weeks of my career." I was sworn to secrecy myself and told absolutely no one at work. I had contacted his wife at one point and told her that I knew what was going on and to contact me if she needed anything. Her response was quite tense, and she only wanted to know how I had known about the situation.

For the next few months, work was quite lonely. I would go in, respond to calls for service, then chill. We were essentially told to stand down, told not to congregate with each other, and were encouraged to keep away from each other to minimize our exposure to the virus. We were experiencing high favorability numbers with the public in general during this period due to the perceived risks we took in performing our jobs, and for the limited time that I knew that goodwill would last, it felt good.

That goodwill lasted exactly until May 25, 2020, when Derek Chauvin, a white Minneapolis, MN police officer knelt on the neck of a subject he'd just arrested, George Floyd, resulting in Floyd's death. Instantaneously, we were public enemy number one. The riots and demonstrations that popped up nationwide were staggering, and the politicians who had ordered all citizens to stand down for months were now perfectly fine with people gathering in large groups to riot and create incredible disorder throughout the USA. I cannot describe the feelings that most of us were experiencing. There was absolutely no one who agreed with what Chauvin did; yet, we were all collectively seen as "racist cops." At one of the protests, eight of us were chosen to be bused over to work crowd control and hopefully ensure that public order was kept. The absolute seething hatred you saw aimed directly at us was palpable. We had not gotten into any physical confrontations, but I had been involved in quite a few mini riots in Atlanta, so I was used to what we had faced that day, although for some, it was quite an eye-opening experience. I could see fear in the eyes of some of the guys/girls I was working with, but it just further enforces the fact that you must be ready every single time you put on that uniform because the question is not if, but when, your day will come.

My father was suffering from Alzheimer's disease and was living in an assisted living facility when COVID struck, so we were no longer allowed to visit him. Then he "supposedly" became sick with pneumonia, and he was admitted to the hospital for a few days before he was brought back to the facility in less-than-optimal shape. We were able to facetime once or twice, and he looked startlingly older in a very short period of time.

Sadly, we received word that he had passed away on April 16, 2020. It was such a weird time in all of our lives as we were unable to hold a wake or funeral for him, and since my mother had him cremated, he essentially disappeared into thin air. After speaking to my mother later the morning my father died, she mentioned that she had already called the Social Security Administration (SSA) earlier that day to check on his death benefits. I knew at that precise point who was running the show, and it wasn't my mother. She would never have dreamt about calling the SSA to inquire about death benefits, especially because she had more money than she would ever need. My intuition told me that the person who was pulling the purse strings was absolutely going to try and claim the entire inheritance for herself, and in the end, that is exactly what had happened.

I had such mixed emotions about my father's passing, truth be told. I did not like him as a man, but he was still my father, and I loved him. I was absolutely thankful that COVID had taken him fairly soon after his Alzheimer's diagnosis since that is one of the most hideous diseases that anyone could ever suffer from. God bless the workers at the assisted living facilities that work in these Alzheimer's wings because I could not imagine having to go to work every day in that environment. It is absolutely one of the most depressing places I've ever seen in my life.

Things started to approach something resembling normality in the fall, although I would not be around long at work to see if it would last.

# CHAPTER 19

September 20, 2020, the day that would change my life for-ever, started out like any other normal day. I had gotten to work for a 3:00-11:00 p.m. tour that evening working my regular 220 car. As I got dressed in the fire house, the dispatcher threw out a call, "on the blind," which means that the sector car who's responsible for that area wasn't available, and no other unit that was close to the location was either, so the dispatcher asks if anyone can handle the call.

In this case, it was a call of a lift assist involving a self-professed 450 lb. woman who had fallen and was unable to get up. The call was in 207's sector, the adjoining sector, just north of mine, so I responded that I would pick it up. Dispatched along with me was a rookie who had seemed like a fairly capable guy from what I'd seen in the limited time that he'd been with us. We arrived at ap-proximately the same time, rang the bell, and entered the home after someone yelled for us to come in.

There we found the caller, a middle-aged woman who weighed quite a bit more than 450 lbs. in my estimation. She explained that she needed help getting up the stairs as she lived in a split-level and was currently on the landing between floors. When we started this process, the rookie ended up in front of her and helped pull her up the stairs while I got stuck behind her and had to physically pick up her right leg to place it on each step as we climbed. The incredible smell that was emanating from this woman cannot be overstated; it smelled like the strongest smell that you could ever imagine of the word that rhymes with "bass."

I don't usually get grossed out by anything, but I almost dry heaved once or twice at that atrocious scent. I glanced up at the rookie, catching his eye, and the message I was sending was, "Your ass should be down here, not mine!" As we crested the top stair, I placed her foot down but realized that it was slipping backwards. I knew in an instant that if she fell down the stairs, she was taking both of us with her. I immediately crouched, then quickly rose up forcing her up the stairs, ensuring that we'd both live to see another day. The problem was, when I shoved her, I felt a lightning bolt shoot through my lower back and knew instantly that I had just injured myself badly. I was proud that I hadn't made a peep after suffering incredible pain but knew something was very wrong.

I gathered all of her information that I needed to complete my report, and we left the home, at which time I advised my co-worker that I had just injured my back in the incident. I telephoned the sergeant's office at the precinct and told my boss what had happened. Thankfully I spoke with Mike Gorey, because he was one of the best bosses that I ever had in my entire career, and I knew I was going to be spending a few hours with him as I had to go to the hospital to be examined by a doctor. I was able to drive to the precinct, and we went to the hospital together. I was in excruciating pain and was given a pain killer in an effort to ease the pain, but it did nothing. I was given an additional pain killer after advising the doctor that the first pill had done nothing to ease the pain.

Then finally, I received an IV pain medication. At that time, I told the doctor that I was absolutely high, but the medicine did nothing to stop the pain. They contemplated giving me an MRI since I was in such excruciating pain, which was rarely done, but now I could not even walk normally to compensate for the back pain. After the doctor decided against that procedure, I was discharged from the hospital, went back to the precinct to fill out some paperwork, and then I was driven home by other on-duty officers as I was unable to drive due to the narcotics that had been administered.

I went to see a neurosurgeon named Salvatore Palumbo in W. Islip, NY, and if anyone in that area ever needs to consult a neuro, I could not recommend Dr. Palumbo more highly. He is incredibly intelligent, his bedside manner is impeccable, he is a gentleman, and most importantly, he believes in conservative treatments before ever resorting to surgery.

I received an MRI shortly after I had seen Dr. Palumbo, and it was confirmed that I had herniated my four lowest discs in the incident. After going through conservative treatments for approximately six months, it was agreed that I would undergo a laminectomy procedure on April 1, 2021. The doctor had told me that several symptoms should be cured after the surgery but that my lowest disc L5-S1 was in poor condition, and a spinal fusion was probably going to have to be performed on me at some point, although we were trying to delay that as long as possible.

I received that surgery and rehabbed enough to the point that I believed I could go back to work, at least light-duty, on the desk in mid-October. It was great to be back with the guys, but it was evident fairly quickly that the surgery did not correct everything that had been bothering me just as Dr. Palumbo had suggested. I was having trouble sitting at the desk, bending over to write or type, and I lasted exactly three days until the pain had become unbearable. I told my wife that I did not want to go back out line of duty with the injury but knew that I would not be able to fulfill my job duties with my back in its current condition.

After going out "line of duty" a second time, it was agreed upon by the doctor and myself that we would proceed with the spinal fusion on March 31, 2022. This surgery was much more intense, totaling five hours, and I was admitted into the hospital for three days. I was not allowed to lift anything heavier than five pounds for approximately four months and was fastidious with my rehab schedule.

The police surgeon told me that I would not be cleared to go back on the streets with a spinal fusion at the age of 54, so I decided to apply for a medical pension, which was granted on October 22, 2022, almost two years to the day that I had been injured. I still had to go through a worker's compensation case regarding the injury, which was finally settled in the fall of 2023. The police department employs a unit that monitors and videotapes officers who go out with line of duty injuries in an effort to catch those who are faking or exaggerating the extent of their injuries. As a result, in addition to not being able to work, volunteer, go to the gym, or pretty much go anywhere with the threat of being video-taped, even getting in my car too smoothly, I found myself having no real purpose.

It was during the latter portion of this time that I found myself getting a little depressed, angry, and experiencing a feeling of overall unhappiness. That is unusual for me. I found that I could wake up feeling great in the morning, but if I had one negative thought, it would begin this vicious cycle of depressing thoughts about anything and everything. I told my wife about it as I'm quite self-aware, but I could not find the origination of these feelings. I remember a couple of times that I just started tearing up which had shocked me as I had absolutely no idea why I was feeling that way.

I had begun lamenting the fact that I was no longer this thing that I was for 30 years, and I was no longer a part of this thing that I had been for 30 years. The brotherhood, for all intents and pur-poses, was gone, out of sight, out of mind. In some respects, I had just disappeared from work, and only a teletype at work, which detailed that I had received a medical pension advised my former co-workers what had happened to me. I was struggling and didn't know why. Even more importantly, I had no idea what I could do about it.

I had opted to apply for Social Security disability and was approved, but this meant I could no longer have a job that paid more than $1,500/month. It sounded great at the time, but what do you do at the ripe old age of 54 when you don't have too many hobbies other than working out? I had been working since the age of 12 and knew that I needed a purpose. I just wasn't sure what it was. To compound the problem, if I found a job that I enjoyed, I would have to notify workers comp and ask permission of them to "approve" the job I wanted. Idle hands are the devil's work, the old adage goes, and I certainly had idle hands at this point. That only gave me more time to think and periodically things would pop up in my head about my former career, thinking mostly about the calls which had affected me mentally, but that I had compartmentalized (BURIED!).

I was sitting at my kitchen table one day when I remembered a suicide call that I had responded to, backing up another unit. Upon entering the home, I saw a man hanging from an oak beam in his kitchen as his brother, who had found him, stood right next to us. A short time later, I was holding up the victim's legs as the coroner's assistant removed the belt from his neck. After leaving that call, the three of us who had responded to handle it said nary a word between us the rest of the day, certainly nothing about that call and how we had each felt.

Another extremely intense call involved a death notification my partner was forced to make after receiving a message to contact a detective from the Myrtle Beach police department. The detective explained that the 20-year-old son of a family that lived in my partner's sector had been in Myrtle Beach for spring break, and while intoxicated, fell to his death after attempting to jump from one balcony to another at a hotel. I'll never forget us turning onto that street as the father was exiting his house. He saw us and immediately dropped to the ground prostrate, screaming, crying as he punched and kicked the ground. We had to break the news to him that his son had passed, and after wailing, he ran into the house, yelling for his wife and daughter. When they came down the stairs, he screamed that their son and brother was dead. You can imagine what took place after that. It was absolutely heart wrenching, and as with so many other calls, after leaving the scene, we basically didn't say a word to one another for the rest of the day.

I could not understand why these traumatic calls were suddenly popping into my head. I hadn't thought about them in years, and for some reason, they were periodically now becoming conscious thoughts. They all had one thing in common though. When I experienced these traumatic events as they occurred in real time, I never processed them. They were compartmentalized (buried) initially, and as they reared their ugly heads once again, I did the same thing, quickly trying to replace them with other thoughts, as the feelings they dredged up were filled with sadness. I now know that sitting with these thoughts, feeling the pain, discovering why they're affecting me so deeply is obligatory in processing and finally healing from that pain. I have only realized in the very recent past that although most of the events I had experienced in my career had initially only appeared to affect those directly involved, many of them hurt me as well.

I was not aware of this reality during my career, but I hope that military veterans, first responders, and frankly anyone, realize through my story that although these tragedies affected those directly involved, secondary trauma is trauma that is witnessed by others. As a former first responder, I had occasion to experience an untold number of secondary trauma incidents. Taken cumulatively, they will absolutely take a toll on your psyche and affect you in a myriad of ways, but many times, you're not even aware that you're experiencing this type of trauma yourself.

I could not reconcile the fact that retirement, which had seemed so attractive a short time before, had taken such a dramatic spiral downwards after becoming reality. I had heard about officers retiring and then becoming profoundly sad and lost, but that possibility had never even been a fleeting thought for me, and I wasn't sure how to get back to my once happy-go-lucky self. I was absolutely sure that I needed a purpose in my life, but was not sure what it was, or how I would go about finding it. How many times have you ever really sat down and thought to yourself, "What do I love to do?" I was asking myself that question, yet I was not yet sure what the answer was.

In between both of my surgeries in April 2021 after three long years of gamesmanship, I had finally gotten divorced. Elise, my then fiancée at the time, and I wanted to get married on September 2, the day of our initial date in 2018, and we did not want to wait almost a year and a half, so we decided to get married on September 2, 2021 (Guys, remember that life hack – You only have to remember that one date the rest of your life) at a beautiful ceremony in front of our friends and family. I knew it was right this time, and I was so proud to be married to this beautiful woman.

She has made me a better man since day one. She's so loving and empathetic and has encouraged me to heal from the various traumas that I've suffered in my life using incredible communication skills. I don't know what I've done in this life to deserve her, but I wish that every man in America could see what it's like to experience pure healthy love from a woman so they know how high that bar can be set. She's helped me learn so much about myself and the origination of certain traits and behaviors and has encouraged me to become introspective and dive into what makes me who I am. She's blessed me with two great stepsons who I truly love, and although I probably don't deserve her, I couldn't be more thankful that we get to spend our lives together.

# THE RESILIENT WARRIOR

# CHAPTER 20

In the middle of trying to work through my own emotional battles, I got a call from my mother one Tuesday afternoon in September 2022. We were chatting casually when she suddenly said, almost as an afterthought, "Oh, I'm in the hospital." Two days earlier, she had woken up jaundiced her skin yellow, her eyes tinted and my sister had rushed her to the hospital but she chose to wait before telling me. When I asked why, she said she didn't want me to worry. That explanation cut deeper than she probably realized, I've always been the one who handles crisis and I stay calm when everyone else panics, even she acknowledged that, so why shut me out?

When the doctors diagnosed stage four pancreatic cancer, my world shifted. She went through a brutal Whipple procedure, months of pain, and chemo so harsh it had to be stopped early. But what added to the weight of all of it was the silence, the filtered communication, the lack of access, the sense that every piece of information reaching me had to pass through someone else's approval first. Every offer I made to help to drive her, sit with her, simply show up was politely deflected. It was as if an invisible gatekeeper decided when and if I would be allowed in. My wife and I put our move to Florida on hold, I wasn't going anywhere, not when my mother might need me. Unfortunately, though the more I tried to get closer, the more I could feel a wall being built between us one brick of secrecy at a time.

Nearly a year later, in September 2023, I received a call from my Uncle Joe who had just visited my mother at a rehab facility in Rhode Island. His voice was uneasy as he urged me without explanation to get an elder-care attorney "to protect my interests," I kept asking what he meant but he wouldn't say. Then moments later, my mother called and told me she needed to see me in person, no details, just urgency.

Worried something was terribly wrong, my wife and I went to Rhode Island. My mother sat across from me and told me with a rehearsed calm that she had bought a house for my sister more than four months earlier. A house, a major life decision, and the two of them had chosen to keep it a secret from me. Not until they were cornered by circumstances did the truth come out.

I wasn't angry about the gift; she had every right to be generous. What shattered me was the calculated choice to exclude me the way decisions were being made around her life while I was kept in the dark. It became painfully obvious that someone had taken control of the narrative and of her. The explanation offered by my sister was disturbingly simple: *"Mommy told me not to tell you."* As if that justified the deception, as if isolating me protected her.

The pain was instant and suffocating a punch to the chest, I felt betrayed by people I loved more than anything. People I had paused my own life for and in that moment, something inside me broke. It's a devastating realization when you see that influence can become manipulation, and love can be used as leverage. Most importantly that the person you're trying hardest to protect may no longer be free to choose who protects her.

Looking back, I know my anger was just armor, beneath it was heartbreak, disbelief, and a desperate desire for someone anyone to understand how deeply their choices hurt me. I tell this story because no matter who it is family, friend, or anyone else control disguised as care is still control. Secrecy is still betrayal, and silence only deepens the wound.

What I needed from my mother wasn't fairness or gifts it was honesty, trust, and the chance to stand beside her when she needed me most. I wish I had found the courage then to say how much I was hurting instead of allowing anger to speak for me. Vulnerability might not have changed their decisions, but at least my heart would have been heard.

After arriving home, I called my uncle and thanked him for looking out for me. He was then able to explain that he and my aunt had offered for my mother to move in with them to recover since my sister's house was less than optimal for a quiet recovery. She had accepted their offer after admitting that it was difficult to stay with my sister for several reasons. They went home after the visit and immediately called their real estate agent to reset the parameters as they would need one more bedroom since they were currently house shopping.

Only a few hours after visiting my mother, and her agreeing to move in with them, she called them and said she had made a mistake, that she was "kidding around," and that she loved living with my sister and she did not want to move in with them. When pressed, my mother accidentally revealed that she had purchased a house for my sister and responded, "No," when asked by my uncle if I had known about it. My uncle told my mother that if she didn't tell me about the house purchase, he would do so. It was that call with my mother accidentally admitting to the house purchase that caused my uncle to call me regarding the elder care attorney. He and my aunt had finally seen what was going on, and the extent of the influence that my sister had over my mother.

In addition to struggling with my post-retirement feelings, I now realized that I had no longer had a family, and my mother although alive, was a shell of her former self. I thank God that I have such a fantastic wife because she was the most nurturing person in the world, and I was experiencing an absolute loneliness knowing that for all intents and purposes, I had no longer had a family. The level of treachery was something that I had never experienced in my life, let alone by my family, and I was just stunned at the level of insidious behavior aimed towards me. I told my wife shortly thereafter that there was no reason for us to stay in New York. If my mother had thought that little of me and our relationship, then why was I even staying close to her geographically?

# CHAPTER 21

In the spring of 2023, while still living in Smithtown, NY, just a few months before receiving the call from my uncle, I had gone outside to watch a podcast episode of *The Shawn Ryan Show*, not knowing that the entire trajectory of my life was about to change. I was still struggling with those feelings of anger, rage, depression, and general unhappiness. I was still unsure of the origination, but unbeknownst to me, I was about to find out.

Shawn's guest for that episode was a man named Eddie Penney, a former member of the Navy SEALs, in fact a member of DEVGRU, or what's more commonly known as, "SEAL Team Six," the Tier one level of the SEALs. During the episode, Eddie began recounting the story of "The Extortion 17 Incident," in which a Chinook was shot down in Afghanistan by insurgents using a Rocket Propelled Grenade (RPG) killing all 38 people on board, including 17 SEALs. It was the largest loss of life in the SEAL community ever, and many of the SEALs were also members of SEAL Team Six.

Killed in the crash was Jason Workman, Eddie's best friend, and as Eddie recounted the story of escorting Jason's body back to his hometown in Utah and then to his final resting place in Arlington National cemetery, he was obviously upset, rightly so. I simultaneously began thinking about the call that I had handled five years before involving Dana, the two-year-old who was found floating in a pool. As Eddie cried while telling his story, I NOW know that

I was subconsciously given permission to cry myself because this absolute warrior was doing so in front of me I began crying like a baby. As it was happening, I had no idea what was going on, in fact, I actually asked myself, "What the FUCK is going on?" Crying is not something that I did, at that point, I had only done so three times as an adult, and all three occasions were when I was forced to euthanize one of my dogs.

Very shortly thereafter though, something clicked, and I said to myself, *"I think I have some sort of PTSD."* I had never entertained that possibility for a second, either during my career, or in post-retirement, but it was becoming fairly obvious to me that the feelings that I had been experiencing were easy to explain when I introduced that diagnosis into the equation. I realized that I needed some sort of help, I did not want to be this ornery guy who hated everyone and everything for the rest of my life. I had seen it plenty of times before and immediately vowed that would never become me.

I began to think of what "getting help" actually meant, and my first thought was traditional counseling or therapy, but I didn't believe that cognitive therapy was going to do it for me. I didn't think that I could speak to some man or woman sitting behind a desk and tell them the things I'd done, and the things I'd seen, and they were going to be able to help me. I've been to plenty of parties where midway through telling a crazy story, I would watch as people recoiled, and realized, *"That's not normal. Let me stop telling this story right now before they begin to think I'm nuts."* Even though a therapist would be much more conditioned and trained to hear the details of traumatic events, I've heard numerous stories of first responders speaking to therapists, and the therapist bursting into tears after listening to them. They may have been ill-equipped to help them, but I personally did not think that any therapist was going to be able to help me in any way, shape, or form. Furthermore, even if they could help me, how long would that possibly take? I didn't want to choose a process that was going to require five years of visits before I saw any type of improvement.

Luckily though, I had seen on Shawn Ryan's as well as other podcasts, special forces soldiers coming home from war, self-professed broken men. They were all recounting stories of their subsequent healing journeys, and many of them had realized profound and cathartic healing after using psychedelics at facilities with personnel who were trained in these sacred ceremonies that have been used for thousands of years. I began to pay close attention to their stories and experiences and started to research these substances myself. I was focusing very heavily on Ayahuasca, a combination of a vine (Banisteriopsis Caapi) and leaves of a tree (Psychotria Viridis), which is prepared by essentially boiling the two ingredients in a pot of water and utilizing the resultant liquid after filtering out the impurities. Dimethyltryptamine (DMT) is the active psychoactive ingredient in the brew and induces intense, often indescribable, subjective experiences involving vivid visual hallucinations, altered sensory perception, ego dissolution, and encounters with seemingly autonomous entities.

When I first became aware of these psychedelics, approximately a year or so before, I had dismissed them as drugs or hocus pocus, but I started paying attention to their seemingly miraculous healing effects after hearing warrior after warrior tell their stories of healing. I knew that these men possessed incredible mental fortitude, yet they described how they became shells of their former selves with seemingly no hope, and then their consequent new life after journeying with these medicines. I soon decided that I was going to travel to South America to journey with these medicines as I was not aware of any accessible treatments in the US since Ayahuasca was classified a Schedule I drug. What I was not aware of was that Ayahuasca is considered a sacrament that can be used in religious ceremonies when obtaining permission through the Religious Freedom Restoration Act.

We decided that we were going to relocate to Florida at the end of 2023, and during my wife's researching of everything related to the move, she had stumbled on a church in Orlando, Fl. called Soul Quest Ayahuasca Church. I was shocked to find that we (my wife decided she would also like to partake) would be able to journey with this medicine in the US after all, and even better, the facility was located approximately two-and-a-half hours away from our new home in Florida.

# CHAPTER 22

After arriving in Florida on December 30, 2023, we made plans to attend a ceremony at Soul Quest on the weekend of March 1, 2024. We gathered more information on what preparations had to be made such as dietary restrictions and what medications or supplements we were supposed to discontinue as even Afrin was frowned upon. Neither of us were ever prescribed SSRIs or anti-depressants, but if we had been, it was imperative that we tapered off slowly and had to discontinue their use for a period of a few weeks prior to journeying with Ayahuasca. That fact was greatly stressed at length, several times. Additionally, we watched a multitude of YouTube videos of people describing their experience with the medicine, and how they implemented changes in their lives, post-ceremony. Although I was full speed ahead in terms of journeying with the medicine, I'd be lying if I said I had no apprehension or wasn't nervous about what I would experience. It was the fear of the unknown, but I had read a quote from someone which read, "Radical pain requires radical healing." I was very willing to give this a try as we had nothing to lose but time and money.

The day finally came. March 1st was upon us, and as we drove up to Orlando, I kept wondering what this weekend would bring. Would it change my life as so many who'd journeyed with medicine said during interviews, or would it all be a colossal waste of time and money? I had no idea at this point, but after hearing so many incredible stories, I was willing to give it a shot and throw caution to the wind.

The facility looked like a normal house in the neighborhood except for a big sign and some flags flying on large flagpoles in the front. After checking in, we were ushered to an office where we were cleared medically by an on-duty paramedic who questioned us about any and everything we had been taking, whether it be natural supplements or prescription medicine. Then our blood pressures were taken, and we received the go ahead to participate in the weekend's ceremonies. We were scheduled to drink later that Friday evening, Saturday morning, and at a third ceremony on Saturday evening. As we were shown around the property by a very nice volunteer, I saw more and more people, both workers and volunteers, as well as other ceremony participants. I was definitely feeling a "Hippie Vibe," and at one point, I asked myself, *"What the fuck are you doing here, bro? These are not your people."* We were there though, and there was no way that I was turning back. Let the chips fall where they may was my thought process. Additionally, after watching so many people on YouTube detail their experience, one theme that seemed to be echoed throughout was that you had to release control in order for the medicine to work. If you "fought it," it would inhibit the medicine from working fully. I was at peace with myself in that respect and told myself that whatever happened, I was not going to fight it.

So, after settling in and getting comfortable, we ate a light snack as you're not supposed to consume any food later than five hours before the ceremony to ensure that you journey on an empty stomach. We all had to attend a mandatory meeting at approximately 4:00 p.m., at which time many things were discussed, including etiquette for the weekend, how the ceremony would unfold, and what we should expect in terms of purging, which is the symbolic act of releasing all things that no longer serve you. We were also told that some people purge by defecating, although you don't lose control, you're able to walk to the bathroom. Everyone told us though, "Do NOT trust an Ayahuasca fart!" We then gathered around the ceremonial space at the back of the property, which contained a large fire pit in the middle. Fire is a big focus of the ceremonies. Additionally, there were alpine style lounge chairs placed in a semi-circle of the yard, and there were two buildings close by, each was approximately 18x40 ft. and they were used by anyone who desired a quiet space while journeying. We all found our seats and were led in spiritual prayers by the staff, who then offered Rape (Ra-Pay), or Hape (Ha-Pay). These substances are finely ground up tobacco that's been used for thousands of years to calm and ground people and is often used to heal physical and spiritual ailments. They are also used in Ayahuasca ceremonies to allow the user to have a deeper connection to the nature and the medicine. I decided that I was going to experience everything in my first ceremony, so I raised my hand to be served.

The process of serving it consists of a shaman, or facilitator in this case, puts the powder into a specialty pipe where it is blown into each of your nostrils. It is not a pleasant experience (at least it was not for either myself or my wife), and I caught a pretty intense buzz rather quickly (sort of like when I dipped Copenhagen for the first time). I sat back in my seat and tried to relax as my nose began to run. I kept spitting my saliva, now mixed with the Hape, into my little trash can that we were each given. I was worried about throwing up, but I managed to not do so, and the effects began to wear off approximately 10 to 15 minutes later. Shortly thereafter, we watched as the staff performed a few chanting rituals. I really enjoyed that they respected the medicine and treated it as something very sacred, which I truly believe it to be. This is not something that gets you "high." There is no euphoric feeling whatsoever, so anyone who is searching for that feeling will be left sorely disappointed. There is a widely held misconception that Ayahuasca is a drug. It is not. It is a plant-based medicine, and it's been used for thousands of years as such.

We were then called to the altar where we formed a line to be served the medicine, and when it was my turn, I was asked if I had consumed before and what my intentions were. I told the facilitator that it was my first time and that I was looking to go deep and was attempting to shed a lot of pain that I was holding inside. After a quick blessing, I was handed the shot-like ceramic cup and chugged the medicine, which is a fairly nasty tasting potion, rich in texture, and a taste that I cannot compare to anything else I've ever consumed in my life. I then sat back in my seat and waited for the effects to kick in.

I had spoken with the gentleman sitting next to me, a very nice guy, who had been to Soul Quest before, and he was seeking some type of message as to the direction his life should be taking. I told him my intentions, and we wished each other a good journey, then began to sit in silence, as did all of the participants after everyone was served. After about the 30-minute mark, nothing had started to happen and negative thoughts started to enter my head. I was asking myself if I had just wasted time and money for nothing, and that they probably had not given me enough. Approximately 15 minutes later, it started! The ground began to move, then I noticed geometric patterns on it and in the sky, which is a very common occurrence for most people that drink. I began looking at the raging fire in the fire pit, and I started seeing the most vivid and dynamic colors I had ever seen in my life. It was absolutely beautiful.

Although the sun had gone down, it seemed like the entire space that we occupied was very well lit when, in fact, the only other lighting besides the fire were strings of round bulbs that hung from the trees approximately ten feet in the air, certainly nothing very bright. I began looking up at the trees, and it seemed as though I was looking at the biggest, most intense forest I'd ever seen, although there were only a few sparsely covered trees there. Then it happened. Most people sense a female presence when they drink Ayahuasca, they call her "Mother," "Mother Ayahuasca," or

"Grandma Ayahuasca," and the plant itself is called the "Mother" plant. Suddenly, as I looked in the sky, it was though I was looking at a big screen television, and "Mother," headdress and all, was in the top left-hand corner looking at me. I didn't even realize that I had done it, but when I first saw her, I opened my arms wide as though I was about to hug someone. I began talking to mother in my head as well as out loud and said, "Please, I need help, help me get rid of this rage, this anger, this hatred. I don't know what to do." And as I said it, I just began crying. I wasn't weeping, but tears kept running down my face, and every time I wiped them away more tears would flow.

The most incredible thing began happening though. Every single time I asked for something, I could feel it being granted, and I felt this weight on my shoulders getting lighter and lighter. What started out feeling like 1,000 lbs., went down to 500, then 250. There was so much going on that I definitely cannot recall it all, but I remember as the ceremony was taking place I was looking around at the volunteers. I like to journey while sitting up. I usually don't lie down at all, and I never close my eyes. As I looked at the volunteers, I was awestruck at their grace, empathy, and love that they showed in helping us. The volunteers, "Hold Space," which essentially means that they're there to serve us in any capacity if we need help during our journeys. I remember telling "Mother" that I wanted to be more like the volunteers. I wanted to have more empathy, sympathy, and love in my heart, and just like that, boom, it felt like it was granted. I remember one of the volunteers had walked by me and in my head, I had said to myself, *I wonder where that MF'er is going?* and not in an angry way. It's just the way I would refer to people at the time, but I scolded myself and thought, *"Why do you have to say MF'er, that's not nice,"* and vowed not to label people like that. I was transforming myself right before my eyes, although I could not fully realize or appreciate exactly what was taking place at the time.

At one point in my journey, "Mother" said she was going to bring my dad to me so that we could talk. I waited as she went to get him, and I felt as though the area was extremely well lit and as though I was standing in front of the biggest, brightest marquee that I'd ever seen. As the ceremony went on, beautiful music played at a consistent volume, but now in my journey, as I awaited what felt like a showdown with my father, the music kept getting louder and louder. In reality, it was not though. I felt as though I was looking down an alley waiting for my father to appear. Then the music just stopped, though in reality it did not, but as it did in my journey, I was looking down this alley waiting for my father to appear for what felt like a minute or two, though it was probably a few seconds.

Suddenly, I realized that he was not going to show up, and I threw my hands in the air and said out loud, "Fucking coward, I knew he wouldn't show. He can't talk about feelings." Suddenly though, I felt that this weight had been lifted off of my shoulders, like everything between he and I that had transpired in the last 54 years had just disappeared. The emotional charge of the memories between us that used to stoke anger had literally zero emotion behind them as I thought about various events.

I had also been struggling with no longer being a police officer after 30 years, coupled with the circumstances of my departure regarding the medical retirement where I essentially just disappeared. I was having trouble finding peace regarding that fact, then I felt like the universe started speaking to me. I never felt God's presence, it was more of the universe itself, and we began conversing. The universe then told me that my time had passed, that I had put my heart and soul into my profession, but I was no longer that thing, and young men could now take the baton and run with it. I was done. I could put it to rest knowing that I had made a difference and just like that, I was instantaneously at peace with having been retired.

There were a multitude of things discussed, all of which I certainly could not remember by the conclusion of my journey, but I had experienced loss three weeks before when two of my former colleagues and friends from the Suffolk County PD had committed suicide a week apart. The sergeant who had killed himself had shot himself in the head in the precinct locker room a week after my buddy, a police officer, had killed himself. I'm unsure if those two events had led to this, but as my first journey was concluding, the universe told me that I was healed from my PTSD.

Healing is not linear, so I will not sit here and profess to anyone that I am this healed human being that wakes up, walks round all day, and goes to sleep with a beaming smile every day of my life, shitting rainbows, but the universe told me that for all intents and purposes I was healed from my PTSD. It then told me that my life's purpose was now to go forth and help other military veterans and first responders heal their PTSD and trauma issues. I replied out loud with a simple, "Okay." I was unsure how I was going to implement that, or what it would look like, but I knew that I had just undergone a transformational life experience. After our initial dose, at approximately 7:00 p.m., we were offered a "booster shot" at approximately 9:00 p.m., which I accepted, and the entire journey lasted about four hours and ended at approximately 11:00 p.m.

I sat in my chair at the official conclusion. Many people stayed in the space afterwards, and the gentleman who had been sitting next to me asked how my journey had gone, to which I told him it was fantastic, and that the universe had told me what my life's purpose was now going to be. He responded with, "Well, THAT'S a good journey." His comment cracked me up. He also asked if I knew what time it was but as I did not wear my watch, I guessed that it was about 3:00 a.m., which had shocked him. He then walked over and asked a volunteer for the time, and you can imagine my shock when he came back over and told me that it was actually only 11:00 p.m.!

My wife had endured a very difficult journey, between the nausea and her initial dose of Hape, which had probably been much too large a dose for a beginner. She needed a quiet space, so she had gone into one of the two buildings and I didn't want to bother her, so I just went back to our room, had a bite to eat, and went to sleep. I was mentally exhausted. She returned a short while later, exhausted. We were attending the 9:00 a.m. ceremony the following morning, so we just fell asleep together.

The morning came quickly, and as we began the morning ceremony, it was evident that only about one-half of the attendees from the night before were in attendance. That ceremony was quite different for me in that there were no hallucinations. It was very peaceful, beautiful, and I felt like one with nature. We managed to eat a little food after the morning ceremony and spoke to quite a few people about our experience thus far. It was incredible that people were so willing to share the most intimate moments of their lives with total strangers; it felt like love embracing you.

We were able to catch a nice nap in the afternoon, then prepared for the evening ceremony that night. Unfortunately, it was forecasted to rain, so it was held indoors. It was again very peaceful, but had a warrior vibe that I felt throughout, and at one point, I was in a room filled with American Indians and we were preparing for battle. I remember one of them putting face paint on me, and the universe telling me that I was, and will always be, a warrior. It did not matter what time period that I would've lived; I would've been a warrior in any of them. The universe told me that it had made me that, and I would always be that. It was very powerful to me.

We woke up Sunday morning and spoke for hours about what we both had experienced. It is not my place to tell my wife's story, so I will not, but we had become much closer after sharing intimate details of our individual experiences, then spoke about our collective ones as a couple. I felt like a new man, with a new purpose in life, and there was just so much to go through and process from the weekend. We took our relationship to the next level after that weekend though.

The following Tuesday night, I sat down and filmed a Facebook live because I knew that I could not be the only man, or ex-officer, who had been struggling with these issues. I wanted to show others who were "going through it" that they were not alone. The Facebook Live ended up being 35 minutes in length and had gotten so emotional for me that I had actually cried once or twice, which shocked me.

I remember going into my house and telling my wife what I had just filmed outside, including the crying portion, and told her that prior to the weekend before, there is no way that I would've ever allowed myself to become vulnerable enough to cry, and if I had done so, I would've been extremely embarrassed. Now though, I was proud for being able to show emotion, and although in no way comparing myself to him, I was hoping that I could do for one person what Eddie Penney had done for me in that Shawn Ryan podcast.

Incredibly, I received four calls the following day, three from buddies of mine who were former police officers who had been "going through it," themselves, including one who had a gun in his mouth in the not-too-distant past, which blew me away. I never would've guessed that of him, but that sounds familiar, doesn't it? The fourth was from a female family friend who had been struggling with some issues, and after taking the fourth call, I came back into the house and told my wife, "This is where I'm supposed to be."

I started to realize that there was an epidemic of people, not just military veterans and first responders who were struggling in life, and for whatever reason, I suddenly felt like I had been chosen by the universe to dedicate myself to helping people change and save their lives. I had no idea why I was chosen, it was not something that I had ever thought about, but through additional journeys with Ayahuasca, as the universe and I conversed, I was told that I had been put through everything in my life for a reason. I was made to look the way that I do, pretty heavily muscled, heavily tatted, and sporting a shaved head, for a reason. This was so that when I enter a room and speak to men/women veterans/1st responders about their trauma issues and problems, I have instant credibility with them. We can smell bullshit a mile away, and I was not some "soy boy," as my buddy Matt Smith likes to say, but an absolute alpha male warrior who would kill or die for anyone in my life with zero hesitation.

I've stepped up to the plate multiple times in my life when that price was a distinct possibility. I had suddenly been given this gift of allowing myself to be vulnerable, to speak to others, and tell them about my biggest missteps in life, about my most profound pain, with the ability to cry about it if that is what struck me, and the additional ability to truly not give a FUCK what anyone in this world thought about that.

Additionally, I decided that I wanted to reach out to the family of Dana Sikorsky, the two-year-old that had been found floating in the pool in 2018, the call which had affected more deeply than any other in my life. I wrote a letter which ended up totaling four pages in length. I had addressed it to Dana's parents, and I finally told them how deeply Dana's accident had affected me. I explained in depth the dynamics of the emotions that I had experienced. I was crying throughout the entire letter as I wrote it, and there were water marks covering at least the entire first page. I explained the visceral pain, guilt, inability to see Dana, and everything that I had gone through. I was in no way feeling sorry for myself; I was more conveying the message that I knew that it was supposed to be me at that call. I did not realize it for five years, but that call was directly responsible for changing the entire trajectory of my life, and through me, Dana was now going to save and change lives.

Mr. Sikorsky responded shortly thereafter, and we spoke on the phone at length as he showed so much grace and compassion as he spoke and updated me on the progress of Dana, which had been incredible. She's progressed much further than the doctors initially thought and though she's still got a long way to go, she is a fighter! It was a very cathartic process, and I could not be more thankful for being given the ability and vulnerability to finally write it.

# THE RESILIENT WARRIOR

# CHAPTER 23

After thirty years in law enforcement, I carried the invisible wounds that so many first responders and veterans do—the accumulated trauma, the sleepless nights, the buried emotions, the anger that never quite left. For years, I thought strength meant pushing through, staying stoic, never showing weakness. But the truth is, that definition of strength nearly broke me. My healing began when I finally allowed myself to be vulnerable—to admit I was hurting and needed help. That moment wasn't weakness; it was courage in its purest form.

Through my healing journey, particularly through the use of psychedelics in a therapeutic, intentional setting I experienced something profound. It was as if the armor I had built over decades was finally stripped away, and beneath it, I found compassion, empathy, and love that had been buried under years of pain and survival. I began to see the world, and myself, through a completely different lens. The anger and hypervigilance that once ruled my days gave way to peace, gratitude, and an unshakable sense of connection to others, to nature, to something greater than myself.

Today, I operate on a higher frequency, one fueled by love, empathy, and understanding, rather than fear or control. My soul feels renewed, and my perspective on life has shifted from surviving to truly living. I now know that real strength isn't in suppressing emotion but in embracing it. It's in having the humility to say, "I need help," and the courage to step into the unknown in search of healing. To every alpha male, first responder, or veteran who's been taught to bury their pain, I'm here to tell you that your healing begins when you drop the mask. Vulnerability isn't the opposite of strength; it's the gateway to it.

We arrived home that Sunday after our weekend at Soul Quest, and I felt like I had been reborn, in a non-religious sense. The feelings I was experiencing were very new to me, but it was as though I was seeing things that I had never seen before. I also now saw things that I had seen for a long time, possibly my entire life, but from a different perspective. Things that used to be important no longer were, and things that I had never thought about suddenly became present thoughts.

My wife had been into this "higher consciousness" realm for years, but it was just never my thing, and suddenly when she now spoke about "Abraham Hicks," and "Manifesting," and "vibrating on a higher frequency," it all suddenly started making sense to me. I had never made fun of her. They were just topics and principles that I did not resonate with, but suddenly, I was absolutely in alignment with this new philosophy. I remember thinking on the previous Friday when we first took a trip around the grounds of Soul Quest that, *"These are not my people,"* and I suddenly realized that, *"Those are my people."* They were my people because they cared and they wanted to help. They were graceful and noble, and they didn't care about the pretense of being strong; they WERE strong. I had always associated strength with physical stature, physical prowess, fighting proficiency, and there's still an absolute place where these traits belong in our respective professions. True strength is also found in helping others, in showing love, and empathy, and compassion towards people. That took real strength, and I decided that I wanted to become a man that held those traits dear.

I wanted to help others heal as Eddie Penney had done for me. He had absolutely no idea, but the fact that he had let himself be vulnerable, exposing his deepest, and most raw pain for others to see was beautiful to me. It inspired me, and I wanted to do the same for others. I say that in the humblest way possible. I did not think I was at the level of an Eddie Penney in terms of being a warrior, but I knew in my heart that I was willing to give everything to a cause higher than myself, and I was now willing to give everything of myself in service to others in a different realm. I considered it a gift, and I live in such gratitude that I had been put in a position of being able to possibly help others. I did/do not take that concept lightly, quite the opposite actually, I've never taken anything more serious in my life. I was just unsure how I was going to go about it at this point. I knew that my life's purpose was crystal clear, how I was going to implement this plan was something that I would now have to figure out.

The first thing I felt that I needed was someone who could help my vision come to fruition, and I felt that I needed some sort of mindset coach. I knew immediately who I would choose for this endeavor, a former Navy SEAL named Taylor Cavanaugh. I had been watching Taylor's YouTube videos since they started dropping in the fall of 2022. Taylor had been a Navy SEAL, but due to his own mistakes, he had been kicked out of the teams and lost his trident. He told the story of sitting in a truck for three days with a sawed-off shotgun, ready to kill himself after a few more missteps. On the third day, he stopped feeling sorry for himself and vowed to "stop being a bitch." Shortly thereafter, he sold everything that he had at that point, flew to France, and literally knocked on the front door of the French Foreign Legion to become a legionnaire, which required a five-year commitment. I thought about his story, this man had lost the thing that he had treasured most in this world, almost took his own life, manned up, then moved to a foreign country where he didn't know the language, leaving everyone and everything that he had previously known behind, because he knew that he had to get his mind and life in order. I knew this was the man that I wanted to work with because, although he self-sabotaged himself, he showed incredible resilience in righting the ship.

I reached out to him in April 2024, and we began working with each other shortly thereafter. I'm proud to now call him a trusted friend and confidante, as well as my mindset coach and he's been incredible at not only helping me create a game plan to accomplish my goals, but he's helped me work through various issues that life has sent my way in that time. One of which was about to hit me like a ton of bricks, and I never saw it coming.

# CHAPTER 24

My relationship with my mother was less than stellar after I had been informed that she had purchased my sister a home without anyone telling me. I thought about other topics which had been broached during that conversation at the rehab facility, during which I had asked her if I had been lied to about anything else, and asked, "Am I still even your medical proxy, or did you both change that behind my back?" She answered sheepishly that I had been removed as medical proxy, and that she had appointed my sister to that position, who had also been granted the sole power of attorney over my mom's affairs. I was again stunned. I told her that it actually made more sense since she lived with my sister, but the lying and treachery was sickening to me.

When I told my mother that my wife and I were moving to Florida, she became irate. She accused me of deserting my family, asking me what kind of man I was to leave my two nieces – who had a father, although he and my sister were going through a divorce. I replied that we weren't allowed to see the kids anyway, so the guilt trip wasn't going to work. When I again told her how deceitful she had been towards me, she actually responded with, "Ah, get over it!" I was literally stunned, but my decision was final, and this only further reinforced the fact that she did not care about having me around. It hurt me to my soul. We went upstate to take my mother out to lunch and to say that she was cold as ice is the understatement of the year, I truly felt like we weren't even related. During lunch, she had dropped her fork and coldly asked, "What are we even doing here?" I stated that I had wanted to see her before we left, and she responded with, "Hmm."

We had been invited back up to New York for my niece's communion in May 2024 and accepted. The night before I received an incredibly bizarre phone call from a neighbor that had lived across the street from me when I was growing up but whom I hadn't spoken to in at least 32 years. She was asking me about my relationship with my mother and sister and kept repeating that, "I want to know who to fight for." I kept telling her that I was not going to discuss my personal life with her, then politely ended the call. I was livid that they had been talking about me behind my back once again but decided to continue with the trip for the communion. The trip did not go well, and we ended up in an argument at the restaurant after the communion at which time, my wife and I left the party. The following week, I received a one-page letter from my mother stating that I had been removed from the trust that she had established a few years earlier. I had expected something like that for quite a while, and she passed away one month later with us never speaking again prior to her death. It was truly an incredibly sad situation, but I know who was responsible for that and that behavior will never be forgiven. I tell all of this because I want to illustrate again that just because they're blood does not make them family. If anyone in your life brings you nothing but strife and negativity, excise that person(s) from your life because life is too short and none of us owe anybody anything, certainly not being someone's punching bag. Shockingly, I found out a week after my mother's death that although they each hated each other, a few weeks before, my ex-wife was contacted by my sister in an effort to get "dirt" on me in case I contested my mother's will. How's that for family?

I struggled with that situation greatly but had a long conversation with a mentor of mine who told me first that you cannot let yourself be a victim, he told me, "You are a warrior, and your mind cannot reconcile the fact that you can be a victim." I had expressed my version of events in a factual manner, I was neither looking for sympathy or acting like a victim, but I agreed with his words. Furthermore, he told me that whatever you are put through in life, thank the universe, there is usually a lesson to be learned if you search for it. Many times, we may never figure it out, others may take years to become clear but try and learn the lesson. Secondly, and more importantly, thank the universe for every experience, even if it causes the most visceral hurt and pain because once you heal, you'll be stronger, more resilient, and mentally healthy, which will allow you to engage in healthy relationships. You'll be able to help others. You will never look for external sources to bring you happiness, or fulfill your life, internal happiness is priceless, and unfortunately, it is not common in our society.

My mother died approximately three weeks later in late June 2024. To this day, I am still stunned that she left this earth essentially disavowing me, and I blame one other person for that, although my mother absolutely took part as well. My wife and I flew up to Connecticut and stayed with my cousin for the funeral mass, during which there was zero contact with my sister. I was involved in none of the planning, and I will not get in depth as to what she did/said to others during that time since we exchanged not even a word between us, and truth be told, God willing, will never again do so again in my lifetime. I was not even able to process her death, I feel like my mom had died a long time before that, having been essentially taken over and manipulated by someone else. I wasn't even sure how to feel about it. Her entire personality had changed, and she had become this cold, hardened individual. When I had asked her about seeing her brother, my Uncle Joe in the months before her death, a man that she'd always had a great relationship with, she gave very terse, cold responses about not wanting to see him, which I'd never heard in my life. It was as though someone else was controlling her every thought.

I've had several psychedelic journeys since was inaugural one in March 2024, but my mother's presence, aura, whatever word you would choose here, has never become present, and I would certainly like to "talk" to her if I could. I do not live with an overwhelming feeling of regret though; I know that I did nothing wrong. I tried to be the best son that I could, and it was just never enough. Many of you reading this have probably experienced this in your lives. I never preach but if you know in your heart that you tried to be the best son, daughter, husband, wife etc. that you are capable of, and it is not enough for that other party, it does not matter what title they possess, you may have to "cut the strings that bind you." Constantly questioning yourself and allowing others to treat you disrespectfully will only bring negative energy to your life, and don't we all have enough of that already?

# CHAPTER 25

As I began working with Taylor and we formulated a game plan of how I could tell my story in the hopes that it might resonate with and help others, I realized that it was going to be a slow process. It had to happen organically; I was not going to immediately begin speaking in large conventions and seminars. We decided to use Instagram as a social media platform, and I simply began by recording reels and stories on my Instagram page, detailing my journey, coupling that with police stories along with words of wisdom to help those men and women who were, "going through it." I hoped that they would identify with me, and hoped that I could give them some hope and inspiration to heal like I had done. I do not want to suggest in any way that I was a "cured" individual who had experienced this linear trajectory of healing, and now felt no sadness, negativity, or failure in my life. I would be the biggest liar alive if I had tried to project that image as truth; reality is far from that.

I have realized incredible healing from my PTSD, but life never stops tossing challenges your way. I experience bad days, sometimes question my purpose, and often ask why I believe that I can make a difference in others' lives, but I do not let that stop me. First responders, military veterans, and the like all experience a collective consciousness in which we essentially hold many of the same beliefs. I set out to dispel some of these myths, such as the accepted fact by most of us that showing/feeling emotion is a sign of weakness, when in fact, the exact opposite is true. Showing and feeling emotion is a sign of absolute strength. The same applies to those who raise their hands and ask for help. That act takes guts. Anyone can let the suffering build within, but it's a warrior who realizes that he cannot do it alone.

It's ironic that with almost everything that we do in life, we'll hire a coach or mentor without hesitation to help us reach our goals, but when it comes to asking for help to heal our mind, suddenly it's seen as weakness, and untold numbers of people have gone to the grave, rather than asked for help. Isn't it the definition of insanity that brave men and women have taken their own lives—leaving behind families who loved them—all because they were afraid that asking for help would make them look weak?"

I was also still processing what I had learned and experienced after my Ayahuasca journey. There were so many things that I now saw differently; it was as though my soul had been touched. I began thinking very introspectively about both my private life as well as my career, and I began to realize that many things that I had perceived as being normal were in fact not. It became clear to me that during my career, I had personally witnessed hundreds, if not thousands of critical and traumatic incidents. The PTS (I don't like using the D, although I do most of the time because most people are intimately familiar with that term) that I had experienced was due to my mind's NORMAL response to the incredible amount of abnormal stimuli (starting with my first hour out of the police academy) that I had experienced throughout the last 30 years.

I began to learn to give myself grace. I began to forgive myself for my biggest missteps in life. I was trying to reach this level of perfection, which was an impossibility, but when I felt short, I always riddled myself with criticism. I learned an extremely important lesson, taught to me by my wife and that is that no one speaks to me more than I speak to myself. I began to change the pattern of calling myself a, "Stupid MF'er" when I made mistakes, and I began speaking nicely to myself. I had read an article, which detailed that constant negative talk lowers self- esteem, motivation, mental health, and limits our potential, while also strengthening the negative neural pathways in our brains. I was no longer going to continue doing that. I was going to speak to myself the way I would speak to someone that I loved, and I realized that one of the greatest acts of courage is learning to love yourself fully. Self-love isn't selfish. It's the foundation that allows us to heal, grow, and love others authentically.

As I began making reels on Instagram detailing my journey and speaking about the important subjects that men/women who were "going through it" needed to hear, I wanted them to know that they were not alone. One of the biggest misconceptions is that we believe that we are alone and no one else understands what we're feeling, when in fact, there is a remarkable portion of the population who battle those feelings every single day. Additionally, we all believe that "Everyone else has it figured out," when in fact, NO ONE has it figured out. People let you see what they want you to see about their lives, some hide it better than others, others let you see nothing, but I promise you that no one has it all figured out. Life ebbs and flows, and during those down times, we all battle the demons.

I quickly started to build somewhat of a following because I think people knew that I was being my authentic self, genuine in everything that I said, and they knew that I just wanted to help. I began to get veterans and first responders from around the nation contacting me, and I spoke to many who were trying to navigate these muddy waters of trauma. A few sought out psychedelic therapies and changed their lives instantly, while others checked themselves in to rehabilitation centers for substance abuse disorders or traditional therapy. I've never experienced a more fulfilling feeling in my life than when someone writes to me and tells me that I helped change their life. It is incredible to be able to help someone feel happiness once again, because you're not only positively affecting that person's life, but the lives of everyone that person is connected to.

As far as I'm concerned, there is no one modality for healing that works for everyone. I firmly believe that ANYTHING that works for you should be used by you. The list is immense, but it includes evidence-based psychological therapies like Cognitive Behavioral Therapy, Prolonged Exposure therapy, and Eye Movement Desensitization and Reprocessing (EMDR). There are psychedelic-based therapies such as Ayahuasca, Ibogaine, Psilocybin, and Ketamine-Assisted Therapy. There are also Mind-Body holistic therapies such as Yoga, Breathwork, Meditation, Journaling, Massage, and Cold Exposure. There are also Community Healing programs such as Peer Support Groups, Family Therapy, or Group Therapy. I urge anyone who speaks to a MD who immediately shuts down any of these modalities, especially the psychedelic therapies, out of ignorance, or having no experience with them, to find another doctor. These are potentially life and death situations, and I believe it is unforgivable for a doctor to dismiss them purely because they're unfamiliar with the true healing powers that they possess, or don't agree with their use because of some type of moral issue. These same doctors have no problem issuing prescriptions for anti-depressants or SSRI's that their patients will typically take for the rest of their lives but never get to the root cause of the patient's problem which led them to take the drugs.

I also decided that I was going to be a huge proponent of plant-based medicines as they had changed my life forever. My wife felt the same and although the facility where we had our first experience, Soul Quest Ayahuasca Church, had closed their doors, we had volunteered there, prior to its closing and had established a few important relationships with former facilitators at the facility. One connection we made was with Matt and Gretchen Smith who had contacted us a few months after Soul Quest closed and informed us that they were going to be opening a church of their own called Earth's Embrace Community Church (eembrace.org). They said they'd love to have us be a part of the church as volunteers. We gladly accepted because we both wanted to be in this "healing space" permanently and had hit it off with them quickly after we had met. Gretchen was phenomenal at our first retreat as my wife Elise suffered through a difficult time during her initial journey. Gretchen had been so gracious and caring towards her that we were blown away, and we met Matt the next time we had attended a first responder/veteran-only retreat at Soul Quest. They're two of the warmest, kindest, most caring people that we have ever met in our lives, and I am honored to call them both friends.

Ayahuasca ceremonies are beautiful to me. Don't get me wrong, there is profound pain being experienced by the attendees. It is not rare to hear people openly weeping or screaming during their journeys. Along with this profound pain, however, comes profound healing and it is not unusual during integration the following day to hear people relate that they had been suicidal as they came to the retreat, but those feelings were now gone, replaced by beautiful and uplifting thoughts which they state they hadn't felt in years! We've met numerous attendees who stated that they hadn't experienced happiness in years and after sitting with Ayahuasca only one time, the fog of depression had lifted, and they were finally able to experience happiness once again.

I wanted to do more though, I literally felt as though I wanted to stand on rooftops and shout to the world that you can change your life with this magical medicine. I did not want to get arrested or fall from a roof, so I nixed that plan, but what I did realize was that I wanted to be able to help more people, and to do that, I had to reach a bigger audience. I decided that I was going to start a podcast, to do for others what Shawn Ryan's had done for me. I wanted to bring on guests, typically military veterans and first responders who have been through the cycle of despair, who've gone through the highest of highs, but also the lowest of lows. I wanted men and women who were, "going through it" to realize that they were not alone; to realize there were many others just like them. I wanted them to be able to identify with my guests, and myself, with the intention of inspiring them and giving them hope, so that they too would raise their hands and ask for help. I know what it is like to feel alone, to believe that no one else understands, to believe that you're never going to conquer this vicious cycle that you experience. What man truly wants to feel vulnerable, to lay his heart bare and expose his pain for others to see? It goes against everything we've been taught about strength. Yet, it's in that very act of vulnerability that true healing begins. Until we allow ourselves to be seen, we remain prisoners of our own silence.

I started The Resilient Warrior Nation podcast in late 2024 to reach a broader audience, to familiarize others with my journey and the journeys of my guests, and to help viewers who are struggling to navigate their roads to healing. I've seen suicide, I'm intimately familiar with the devastation that it causes for everyone involved, and I want to use whatever resources I've been given by the universe to help stop it. In various journeys with ayahuasca, the universe has told me that it's put me through everything that I've gone through, both good and bad, for a reason. That reason is so that when I enter a room and I speak to vets/first responders that I have credibility. Professionals in these fields smell B.S. a mile away, and they know instantly whether you're a genuine person who is there to help, or if you're a fraud who's trying to peddle his/her wares. I've walked the walk for 30 years, so now I can talk the talk, and there is an absolute level of trust between myself and ANYONE that I've spoken to since I started down this path of helping others.

I constantly ask myself, "Who the fuck are you to be telling anyone anything or to be giving advice?" I shut that thinking down quickly though as I cannot let it stop me from staying on course. I was told by friends that I am Mike Morgan, that I try to tell no other story other than my own, and I try to be no one else other than my true authentic self in the hopes that my message resonates with those I'm trying to reach. The support that I've gotten is incredible, but the self-doubt is an ever-present emotion. It is normal to feel this way, these feelings are incredibly common, especially among high-achieving people and those who've gone through major transitions, such as leaving a career in law enforcement or the military. When it precludes you from moving forward and accomplishing your goals, however, that is a problem.

How can you overcome these things? First by speaking to yourself differently, reframing the thought from, "I'm not qualified for this," to "I'm still learning, and I've earned the right to be here." For anyone thinking of joining this space, you have decades of high-stress experience and service, now use that to help others heal. Do not compare yourselves to others—we ALL do that periodically. Focus less on how you measure up to others and more on why you're doing the work. When your mission becomes the focus, your doubts become much weaker. People who push through self-doubt take small, consistent steps when they feel uncertain. Each time you act, despite doubt, you train your brain to see that you're capable. Speak to mentors and peers who you trust and tell them how you're feeling. They will tell you your worth when your perception gets distorted. I recently read a meme which stated that our brains lie to us constantly; we are not passive observers of reality, we are the narrators. Our brains invent stories that feel true but often are built on cognitive bias, emotional residue, and past wounds.

Additionally, I "accidentally" realized that my mind was playing tricks on me recently due to hormonal fluctuations. I was feeling sad, unworthy etc. a few weeks ago, but there was no clear explanation for this. Everything had been going relatively well in my life. I remembered that a friend of mine had mentioned that if his estrogen levels spike during his TRT (Testosterone Replacement Therapy), he gets very emotional. I realized that might be the cause of the negativity I had been feeling. Sure enough, after taking my anti-estrogen blocker, I was back to feeling normal less than a week later. I had never realized how imperative and sensitive the hormone levels were in affecting my psychological state. The TRT therapy has been an absolute life changing protocol for me, and I highly encourage every middle-aged male, especially men who worked in high-stress environments, to get theirs checked periodically. The testosterone levels of first responders and veterans are often exposed to prolonged stress, both physical and emotional. When cortisol (the stress hormone) remains elevated for long periods of time, it suppresses testosterone production. This results in men experiencing low energy, low libido, mood swings, weight gain, and slower recovery from physical exertion. We mistake burnout for hormonal imbalances and many times, the cause is physical, not the mental side where we often lay blame.

# CHAPTER 26

As I've begun this healing journey and next phase of my life, I often speak to men, some women as well, but the overwhelmingly majority of first responders and military veterans that I interact with are male. I'm often asked for methods of dealing with these various traumas and how to avoid becoming a statistic or falling prey to PTSD and trauma issues themselves. This is a tricky question because there is certainly no one, or "fool-proof," method to avoid these pitfalls. They usually occur over long periods of time, and you cannot just cross your fingers and hope to not become a victim yourself.

People often hear my story and ask, "Was it worth it, and would you do it again?" My answer to both of those questions is, "In a second!" I would not trade my career for anything, even knowing what I now know. It's been the most rewarding thing I ever could've imagined, and the good I've done certainly outweighs the bad I've experienced. I do have more than a few recommendations to help you avoid some of the pitfalls that I've gone through, and hopefully they can help you realize a long, successful career. Some of these were touched on in an earlier chapter, but here are additional methods to help you throughout your career. I hope you employ many of them from day one. It is not a question of "If" in your career, but "When," and the "When's" include a broad category of issues, such as when you're going to be fighting for your life, when you're going through profound trauma, when a co-worker is going to commit suicide, when you look in the mirror and don't recognize the person staring back at you, when you retire what does the next phase of your life look like? There are many other "When's" that you're going to have to face in these professions, so prepare in advance for as many as you can.

If you've chosen one of these first responder/military professions, know that exposure to trauma is inevitable. You will see things that are not normal, and most people couldn't imagine. You will also carry burdens that go unspoken. Trauma itself does not lead to PTSD; you cannot control what you will witness in these fields, but there are powerful ways to fortify the mind, body, and spirit against the cumulative effect of trauma. The key is not toughness. THE world's strongest men from a mental fortitude perspective cannot defeat trauma and its impacts. The key is balance, awareness, and connection.

## Communication

Communication is the number one method of combatting the devastating effects of trauma. The MOST dangerous words in our vocabulary are, "I'm fine." Bottling our emotions is what allows trauma to grow roots. Talking, whether to a co-worker, family member, friend, therapist, or chaplain helps release the emotional pressure before it hardens into psychological injury. Departments need to prioritize this, and if they don't, the supervisors of individual units must carry the torch. Open conversations, peer groups, or critical incident debriefings drastically reduce PTSD risk. Learning to speak your truth without shame can be the single most protective act of self-care, healing starts when we replace isolation with connection.

## Physical Fitness

Physical fitness is not just about staying fit; it's medicine for the nervous system. Trauma lodges itself in the body through tension, inflammation, and disrupted energy flow. Exercise releases hormones like cortisol and floods the brain with dopamine, serotonin, and endorphins—the natural antidepressants and anxiety regulators. Physical exercise can help reset the body's chemistry. The goal is movement with purpose, physical exertion that sharpens the mind and releases emotional pressure. Exercise also increases testosterone and growth hormone levels which were discussed earlier.

## Nutrition

Processed foods, sugar, and alcohol all increase inflammation and destabilize mood. A clean diet which includes lean proteins, healthy fats, fruits, and vegetables keep the gut and the brain aligned. The gut produces much of our serotonin and maintaining gut health through whole foods, probiotics, and hydration has a direct effect on emotional balance.

## Sleep

Sleep deprivation is one of the most destructive forces in the first responder and military world. Shift work, adrenaline dumps, and late-night calls wreak havoc on our circadian rhythms. Deep sleep is when the brain heals, however, it processes memories, restores hormones, and resets emotional regulation. Those struggling with insomnia often replay traumatic memories because their brain never completes the "filing process" of REM sleep. Maintaining a routine sleep schedule, limiting caffeine, and using techniques like breathwork or meditation can dramatically reduce PTSD risk. For those of you who fear that you may have, or those who DO suffer from sleep apnea, like me, I urge you to get tested if you haven't been. If you've been diagnosed, use your CPAP machine every day of your lives as that condition can wreak hell on your body and mind if not treated properly. Sleep is a tool for mental readiness and life, not a luxury.

## Substance Use

For too many of us in uniform, alcohol takes the edge off or helps us get sleep, but the worst thing that you can do for sleep is use alcohol as it disrupts your REM sleep levels, spikes anxiety, and lowers testosterone and serotonin levels. True healing begins when you face your pain sober and allow yourself to process emotions authentically. Sobriety will give you freedom.

## Support System

Isolation is the absolute worst thing you can do when you're trying to heal from trauma. Building a network of trusted people including friends, family, co-workers, mentors, or support groups will help create a safety net which will prevent you from falling that far when you're dealing with issues. A healthy support system holds you accountable, encourages vulnerability, and reminds you that asking for help is not weakness, it's wisdom and strength.

## Mindset & Meaning

Creating mindfulness through things such as meditation, breathwork, prayer, or spending time in nature helps calm the nervous system and bring awareness to emotions before they spiral into trauma responses.

Purpose driven reflection asking, "Why do I serve?" or "Who am I outside of this uniform?" helps prevent identity loss after retirement or injury. Many who struggle post-career do so because they no longer feel useful or connected to a mission, but reconnecting with service can restore that sense of mission.

## Professional Help

Despite various stigmas, therapy is still one of the most powerful tools for prevention. Trauma-based therapists can help process trauma before it becomes deeply embedded. Psychedelic therapies, which I've used to heal are incredible, and recent studies have proved their effectiveness.

## Purpose

We are purpose-driven individuals, and the healthiest first responders and veterans are those who discover purpose after their service concludes. Whether it's teaching, mentoring, rescuing animals, coaching, or starting a foundation, purpose transforms pain into power. When you align your energy with something meaningful, trauma loses its grip. You stop living in the past and start building your future.

# CHAPTER 27

As I look ahead to the future regarding who I am and what I would like to accomplish, I am excited at what the future holds in store for me. I never would've predicted that I'd be involved in mental health awareness, and I certainly would've never guessed that I'd ever be a huge proponent of psychedelics, or that I would host a podcast, OR write a book, yet here we are! I thought long and hard about writing this book before I ever typed one word of the manuscript.

I often deal with "imposter syndrome" and question my value and relevance in this space that I now occupy. This, even though I try to be no one other than my authentic self, as I tell no one's story other than my own. I do this in an attempt to help others avoid some of my mistakes and to allow them to learn how to heal themselves, or at least present modalities and strategies to do so. I wrote this book with the intention of doing just that, in addition to helping anyone who reads it navigate some of the landmines that I've unfortunately stepped on.

My intention is to get on stage, speak with first responders about real-life examples of potential encounters and calls they may face, ones that I have faced, and methods of winning each and every one of them. I also would like to offer insight on how to process the trauma that you WILL inevitably experience daily so that you do not make decisions and life choices that are detrimental to your well-being. My intention is not to get on a stage and proceed to tell men and women that when first responders experience chronic stress over years, the brain's stress-response system becomes over-activated, the amygdala (fear center) grows more reactive, the hippocampus (memory and emotional regulation) can shrink, and the prefrontal cortex (decision-making and impulse control) becomes less effective. Prolonged release of cortisol, the body's main stress hormone, along with adrenaline and norepinephrine, can disrupt mood, sleep, memory, and immune function, keeping the brain and body in a constant "fight-or-flight" state even at rest.

All of that is 100% true, but I don't believe that "my people" necessarily care about the clinical explanation regarding the processes of stress and its effects on the human body. The overwhelming percentage of people want confirmation that they aren't crazy, that they aren't alone, and that there is help available to them as they attempt to heal their "broken" minds. I want to state once again that what we first responders/military veterans experience is NOT NORMAL. The stimuli that we're exposed to daily for months, years, decades, and finally, entire careers are incredibly caustic, but our body's response to these stimuli is 100% normal. We beat ourselves up about our inability to handle and process these incidents, but how can you successfully complete something that you were never taught to do?

It is my hope, mission, goal, to help as many people as possible become aware of the abnormality of their exposure, and the consequent pitfalls they will experience in attempting to deal and heal from this trauma, but it's almost impossible to do so unless you raise your hand and ask for help. I want to normalize men allowing themselves to become vulnerable, which is a necessity when trying to process and heal from trauma.

Allowing myself to become vulnerable is undoubtedly the single biggest gift that psychedelics has given me, and if it was not for psychedelics, I am all but certain that I would have NEVER been able to heal myself. If you cannot look in the mirror and let yourself be vulnerable, how can you ever be honest and acknowledge that you are hurting, and that you are going to require help to heal? Raising your hand and asking for help is an absolute sign of strength, not weakness, but we have a long way to go before that credo becomes mainstream amongst the internal dialogue of most men.

Had I never watched the Shawn Ryan podcast episode that I alluded to earlier; I can state with absolute certainty that I would be in the same place mentally that I found myself for the year preceding that show. I certainly would not have written a book, created a podcast, have changed the lives of anyone else, and I am fairly certain that I would yet to have healed at all from the trauma that I had experienced in my early life and throughout my police career. I literally owe all this progress that I have made in my life in the past 1 ½ years to a man who doesn't know me from a hole in the wall.

Fortunately, though, Eddie Penney allowed himself to be vulnerable enough to show me that being vulnerable is not weakness, it is how a "real man" processes tragedy and heartbreak. It is my life's purpose to illustrate that principle to as many people as is humanly possible in my remaining years on this earth. Thank you in advance for reading my story and if this book helps just ONE person, my mission is accomplished. For those of you who choose to ask for help, I applaud you for raising your hand and promise you that you will never regret it.

# THE RESILIENT WARRIOR

# ACKNOWLEDGMENTS

I want to thank my beautiful wife Elise, as I truly do not have any idea what I've done in life to have been given such an incredible gift of having her by my side from day one of our meeting each other. I would love for EVERY man in the world to experience the love that she gives me for even just one day so that they could take away from that what a healthy, loving partner feels like, and shed any relationship that does not afford them what I live daily!

To those men and women military veterans and first responders who are "going through it," I PROMISE you that there is hope and healing to be found, you just have to raise your hand and ask for help—I did. You will be shocked at how many people out there actually love and care for you. You will realize how many people want to help you get healthy and happy again, because life is beautiful and you can, once again, experience everything that it has to offer in all of its splendor.

# ABOUT THE AUTHOR

Michael Morgan is a retired law-enforcement professional with over 30 years of service, having served with both the Atlanta Police Department and the Suffolk County Police Department. Throughout his career, he worked in high-stress environments that demanded strength, composure, and resilience—often at the cost of emotional well-being.

After confronting his own struggles with trauma and identity beyond the badge, Michael committed himself to understanding healing, personal growth, and what it truly means to be a warrior after the uniform comes off. Today, he is the host of *The Resilient Warrior Nation* podcast, where he amplifies the voices of first responders, veterans, and leaders who have transformed adversity into purpose.

Michael now dedicates his work to helping others realize that strength is not found in silence—but in the courage to heal.

www.ingramcontent.com/pod-product-compliance
Lightning Source LLC
Chambersburg PA
CBHW071748120626
46550CB00002B/707